Debra Dank's *Terraglossia* is an essential, compelling work that challenges entrenched narratives and celebrates the richness of First Nations language and culture. With meticulous research and a clear, accessible voice, Dank reclaims the power of words to shape relationships and defy colonial oppression. This book goes beyond just language; it captures the personal and community stories that shape research, and advocates for a future rooted in respect, understanding, and self-determination for Aboriginal peoples. *Terraglossia* is not only a scholarly triumph, but a vital call to reimagine how we engage with the world's oldest living cultures. A beautifully written and thought-provoking masterpiece, this book is a must-read for anyone seeking to deepen their understanding of what it is to live, speak and listen on Aboriginal land.

– Evelyn Araluen, award-winning author of *Dropbear* (UQP, 2021)

Dedication

This is for my paternal grandmother, Pbirrianjulunga – ankami ngiya.

About the author

A Gudanji/Wakaja and Kalkadoon woman from the Barkly Tablelands in the Northern Territory, Dr Debra Dank is an Enterprise Fellow with the University of South Australia. She has spent 40 years working in primary, secondary and tertiary education roles, in urban and remote areas across Queensland, New South Wales, Victoria and the Northern Territory. She is interested in multiform narrative and its practice in Aboriginal and non-Aboriginal communities and the role semiotics plays in that. Her book, *We come with this place*, won numerous honours in 2023, including four New South Wales Premier's Awards and the Australian Literature Society Gold Medal. Debra is passionate about the environment, especially as her Country, on the Beetaloo Basin, is under threat of being fracked.

Dr Debra Dank

Terraglossia

noun

1. *earth speak*
2. *tongues of the earth*

antonym: terra nullius

echo
PUBLISHING

Echo Publishing
An imprint of Bonnier Books UK
6/69 Carlton Crescent
Summer Hill NSW 2130
www.echopublishing.com.au

Bonnier Books UK
HYLO, 5th Floor,
103–105 Bunhill Row
London EC1Y 8LZ
www.bonnierbooks.co.uk

Echo Publishing acknowledges the traditional custodians of Country throughout Australia. We recognise their continuing connection to land, sea and waters. We pay our respects to Elders past and present.

First Nations peoples are advised that this book contains names of deceased people and content that may be considered culturally sensitive.

First published 2025

Printed and bound in Taiwan by Choice Development, Inc.

Editor: Anna Rogers
Page design and typesetting: Shaun Jury

A catalogue entry for this book is available from the National Library of Australia

ISBN: 9781760689803 (hardback)
ISBN: 9781760689810 (ebook)

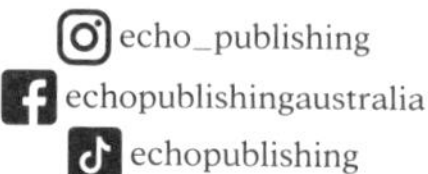

Acknowledgement

I acknowledge and honour the efforts of my parents, my Elders and grandparents, and the old Gudanji and Wakaja families, all of whom have made it possible for me to learn who I am and how I am.

This book is a small but personal tribute to the Ancestors who, in the time of the creation, took breath, created our Country and us, and who, in that big work, began the stories that continue to guide and nurture.

Foreword

I am writing this while travelling through regional New South Wales by train. I kept the reading of *Terraglossia* for this train trip – a gift of words I wanted to slowly unwrap and consume as I travel – and have just finished reading.

Out of the window on both sides I can see the big Australian sky everywhere, white frothy clouds pouring over the horizon, pitching towards us. Erratically sloping plains fringed by hills and craggy cliffs; boulders hunkering, strewn in fields as if left behind by some giant entity. Scattered, beautiful trees, mainly gums of differing varieties, stand toweringly tall, shimmering in the breeze. And black cows staring benignly at the noise we create as we speed by.

Then my eyes are drawn to the fencing throughout this space – everywhere I look, I see fences, low, barbed wire fences, corralling and owning and dividing. They are ugly and fierce – I know they are economic tools of organised agriculture, but they are jarring among this beauty. The spaces they divide were once full of more of those scattered, beautiful, languorous trees, but the land is cleared, the flora and fauna decimated. We call it 'progress' and I am thoroughly aware that as a white middle-class academic, my immense privilege is deeply entangled in it.

This ownership.

This taking.

I watch the tarmac road running alongside the train track, and the track itself leaving the road, then winding and wending its way over the land, through the land, up the hills and around the mountains. I look for animal life and apart from the many black crows see scant, except for the swooping of a white cockatoo here, a magpie over there. I know there are more creatures out there, cunningly camouflaged, or perhaps up the mountainside, away from the clanging and clashing noise we are making, waiting for dusk to fall to venture further afield in the quiet of night.

I think of the paradise this land must once have been. The abundance it provided. The stillness of a morning, waiting for the winds to disturb the hush, the peace, the calm of its people, and the more-than-human, swirling around them all.

It is not lost on me that in this foreword, I am writing in the language which Dr Debra Dank most respectfully announces is inadequate. The irony of that. And I truly believe her. Read this text and you will also understand. It is there, printed on the page: *terraglossia*, the antonym of terra nullius, and I am now deeply schooled more than ever in a parallel ancient truth of this country I call home. That Debra Dank calls home. That her family calls home. I knew it before reading, but not at this profound level.

I am so in love with the title *Terraglossia* for three reasons: one, for its audacity; two, because, potentially, it is one simple step forward in a long history of overt and covert injustices; and three, because of its etymology. And that is where I smile and nod to the genius of author and scholar Debra Dank.

Let me begin with the audacity. Why *not* create a word to oppose a more than 250-year-old assumption of emptiness? Terra nullius was, simply, a lie; an early and devastating piece of 'fake news'. And deeply convenient for the colonising regime back in Britain, which mandated orders that were bombastically and brutally carried out to the letter by troops and settlers then and into the future.

The second reason? It is a word that possibly can give us a way ahead. A simple rectifying of that story; an amendment. If/*when* this one small word is adopted into this English language of ours, the beginning of the healing it could perform is almost unimaginable.

And finally, its etymology. For a semiotician whose second language is English, Dank's creation of a word rooted in *Latin* to combat and oppose and disrupt the long-standing narrative of terra nullius is an exercise in virtuosity. I smile every time I think of it. The satirical cleverness. The irony. The incisive mischief.

I have the deep privilege of calling Debra Dank my friend, and have heard her talk, on Zoom, over coffee, across the table during meals, of her theories and musings about the English language and the damage it causes; the destruction it maintains and prolongs; the near elimination of an ancient and sustainable civilisation. Because do not think for one moment that the First Nations did not live in organised, sophisticated and efficient societies, by definition civilisation.

How could we not see? How did we *choose* not to see?

An example. Dank writes: 'We were, and in some parts of Australia still are, speakers of many languages and dialects, and anywhere else in the world, those speakers of multiple languages would be celebrated as the polyglots they truly are.' This is gut-wrenchingly true. Instead, many believe some First Nations are illiterate, even those with three, four or five different languages. She tells us there was an additional, invisible invader on the First Fleet, hidden but devastating: the English language in all its binary aggression. It is one thing to subvert what non-Indigenous see and feel and live and take for granted as 'ordinary' into an antagonistic foe. But read this book and learn what harm the English language in its self-righteousness has done to our First Nations – to the children, still today.

Dank writes of polyvalency, polyphony and polysemy, three words of such importance in her account, explaining each simply and clearly; explaining how they perform in her world – and how they do not intuitively perform the same way throughout the dominant culture. This is enlightening; the inversion of an epistemic understanding we are not even aware of in our blinded entitlement. This is a forensic detailing through a linguistic lens of what we did so criminally wrongly when we first landed on this continent, what we continued to do and still do today. Read this book and, as in Dank's first, *We come with this place*, learn from these words, written with compassionate graciousness, tinged with a touch of anger and frustration.

But it is the graciousness that is so searing here. Dank explains why she believes the settler violence, meted out so easily, *was* so easy; people ripped from their homeland as felons, even for menial affray, and sent to the other side of the world. Their hardship and their fear. Their quest to survive. She figures this is why the violence towards First Nations became endemic, so quickly and seemingly effortlessly.

She does not blame but carefully tries to lay out the different ways of being a First Nations citizens in contemporary Australia; a First Nations child in one of our schools – and what we as a country are missing out on by ignoring this difference. How we can nurture and grow it, and discover a better way to live together, with respect.

It could be too late to truly reverse what has happened here through policy and ignorance and uninformed fear. But the First Nations of this country will always exist. There is 60,000 years of history flowing through their blood and a way of knowledge-making and sense-making – being – that will never cease. Dank asks the question: If we name Egypt and Greece as 'ancient' 5000 and 3000 years ago, what is the word for our own First Nations, 60,000 years ago? There is no word in the English language to contain this immensity; the question conjures erasure.

But the erasure has not worked, simply because of the different way of First Nations belonging and being. These pages evoke this collective strength, formalised into English so we can understand. There is richness and nourishment and elegant craft here to be shared, so that we can come together and be stronger as a people, jointly. We need only to look through Debra Dank's eyes as she literally spells it out for us, in 'black marks on a white page', in this, her latest gift to the nation.

Associate Professor Sue Joseph
University of South Australia

A note: When I am identified as Aboriginal, Indigenous, First Nations or First Peoples, something of who I am as Gudanji/Wakaja is irrevocably lost, as if washed away in a flood of muddied water, mixing and churning everything together in its consuming wake. I understand that, for the purposes of national conversations, policies and such, labels like Aboriginal and Torres Strait Islander, Indigenous, First Nations or First Peoples are necessary for reasons of expediency. I have used Aboriginal, Islanders, Indigenous, First Nations or First Peoples interchangeably, for the sake of that expediency, to maintain a fluidity of identity and allow room for others to self-identify, and to not cause further loss to others whose ancestors have been here for thousands of years. These terms do not, however, include the knowledge, histories and ancestors of my Gudanji/Wakaja person.

The moving tide – an introduction

In April of 1770, a moving tide brought into what is now known as Botany Bay, a single barque, a British Royal Navy vessel built in the style of a Whitby cat. HMS *Endeavour* sailed under the command of Lieutenant James Cook. The local Dharawal people of Kamay challenged Cook and it is recorded that they did not want to interact with these newcomers. Despite this clear lack of welcome and the obvious occupation, Cook claimed Dharawal land and the lands of all other first nations across this continent for Britain in the name of the British king. As recorded in the *Secret Instructions for Lieutenant James Cook Appointed to Command His Majesty's Bark the Endeavour 30 July 1768*, Cook had been charged with several secret orders from George III, including 'with the Consent of the Natives to take possession of Convenient Situations in the Country in the Name of the King of Great Britain'. This direction he ignored, and that set in motion more than 250 years of ignoring Aboriginal presence and all that entails.

Several years later, Captain Arthur Phillip sailed to what is now known as Australia with 11 ships comprising the First Fleet and set up a penal colony on 26 January 1788. Phillip had proposed to treat Aboriginal peoples well and with consideration, but as with the directions from King George III, many of the plans for the 'discovery' of this place had gone awry. I cannot help wondering what and how the thinking of those first new Australians, rejected and ejected from their own country so violently and transported to a place that had only become a solid reality in the awareness of most British people several years before, contributed to what would occur here. I cannot imagine the terror and the fear of that journey, but I do imagine that perhaps some of these deeply turbulent emotions made the violent aftermath of those landings possible.

The landing of Cook and his subsequent claiming of others' lands, and the actions of those who came after him, continue to have significant, mostly detrimental, effects on the First Peoples. The life-altering events that have affected all Aboriginal populations since Cook's arrival have generally motivated this book and are alluded to in some places, but it is primarily about communicative form and function and how this influences the interactions of Aboriginal and non-Aboriginal people. There was an item of cargo in the company of those who came here on that first cat that continues to grow almost unchecked. It was in the form of a new language, a language that had not visited the shores of this continent and which continues to struggle to articulate the broader context of what had evolved here for thousands of years. There is an urgent need for a big conversation, and a recognition that, in the interests of truth telling, is long overdue; and it seems, to me, that the elephant in the room, or the 800-pound gorilla, but realistically, that clandestine passenger on the Whitby cat, is slowly squeezing the breath from its more than ancient–new Australian body.

With the levels of flora and fauna species extinction, Australia has achieved the dubious title of highest rate of mammal extinctions in the world, achieved since Cook's arrival. There is an ongoing disregard for the 'natural world' and a seeming dedication to taking everything that it is possible to remove from the environment without consideration for the wellbeing or welfare of future populations. Our leaders are swayed by the immediacy of economic gains and the politicisation of protecting the geographic space. It is hardly surprising, then, that care for and consideration of the first human populations of this continent is so haphazard and piecemeal.

That oft-quoted phrase, 'History is written by the victors', is specifically about wars being fought and lost and the motivations for such tumultuous events. The endeavours of First Peoples in protecting communities, families and Country were acts of war in response to the difference in political, civil, social, economic and territorial ideologies newly arrived here. The recordings of these activities have generally been written by others, not Indigenous peoples. Many have denied that wars did in fact occur here on Australian soil while we remember Australian participation in wars on the shores of other places. I think, however, that it may well be better and kinder to our national psyche and global standing to admit to wars being fought here rather than the other explanation for the sheer depth of violence and shattering outcomes to both population numbers of the First Peoples and to our living conditions on the Australian continent.

It is widely accepted that the Aboriginal population size would have been around a million at the time of invasion. Surely, an acknowledgement of war is better than admitting to the depravity that I imagine is necessary, and makes it possible, for an original population size to be reduced from that figure to the 116,000 people who the Australian Bureau of Statistics claims identified as Aboriginal or Torres Strait Islander in the 1971 census. After 201 years, that data suggests more than 884,000 people had lost their lives, because Aboriginal births had occurred in those two centuries, which contributed to the 1971 number. What other explanation can there be for almost 85 per cent of the population to be missing after 200 years of 'repopulating'? And to frame that in a way that may be better understood, statistics tell us that more than half of the Jewish population of Europe was murdered in the Holocaust. I quote one of my favourite authors now because I cannot conceive of any other way to respond to those facts: Kurtz in Joseph Conrad's *Heart of Darkness* saying, 'The horror. The horror.'

A particular tone to the contemporary and historical tellings of those times still exists across this present-day Australian nation. That tone is one of taming a landscape, the rugged and wild landscape and all that is located within it, and there is a carefully structured and worded and oft-told tale about creating the nation. These stories all reflect and represent a single version of the broader truth of this place, which elevates one part of Australian society through the denial of the other. There is also an awareness, but one of which as a nation we do not speak, perhaps because of the pain, that in the clearing of the landscape, people, too, were cleared. There is a carefully maintained overt ignorance of the culturally derived diversities that exist between Aboriginal Australians, and absolutely between Aboriginal Australians and non-Aboriginal Australians.

I believe that some explanation for this can be found beyond those narratives and can be understood when the language itself is examined. Narrative, story, account and tale all describe approximately the same thing – the sharing of an event, in this case, with words through utterance.

There is a common primary school refrain – 'Sticks and stones may break my bones, but words will never hurt me.' Although words do not have the capacity to brandish those sticks, they can indeed narrate a story that might be damaging to those doing the telling and certainly to those about whom the telling is told.

For some time now, as a nation, we have seemingly challenged those attitudes and behaviours that reflect the privileging of one group over another. We have debated the presence of racism, prejudice and bias, and attempts, at much expense, have been made to address the inequities that are experienced by Aboriginal Australians, but such work has resulted in limited success or improvement of the conditions of the first populations of this continent. We have not, however, focused on the very thing that is at the heart of this new Australian national community – words, and the ways in which we use them, and the mechanisms that govern the communication between Aboriginal and non-Aboriginal peoples. I find that to be a tantalising circumstance. A language new to this place, in fact, a language just new, trying to engage with the world's oldest continuous lived civilisations. This, then, is what this writing is about.

In 2022 my first book, *We come with this place*, was published. It was born of one half of my PhD study. Much of this conversation, and I hope it will be a conversation, is derived from the second half of that study. Some parts may be challenging or perplexing but I hope they are also stimulating and thought provoking, because I am presenting Aboriginal people and our communities in ways that non-Aboriginal people rarely see us. I am presenting some theoretical underpinnings of my own Gudanji/Wakaja community. (I expect there are more similarities than dissimilarities with other Aboriginal communities, but I have no authority to speak for them.) I do hope, however, that this sparks further discussion and insider research to further claim a place within the great philosophical traditions of the world because the Ancestors deserve that, at the very least.

There is much knowledge contained within the claim of being the oldest continuous lived civilisations in the world. There is much to be shown and told and illustrated, and much of it lived, and lives still, outside that institution in which I have spent such a large part of my life. Aboriginal knowledge lives in the people and the environment and in the relationships with our non-human kin, but the explanations and definitions needed to expose that knowledge must be told through our thinking ways, through our philosophical underpinnings and not in a translated mode of telling. I hope that all of what I offer in this book will reveal some of the big but different ways that Aboriginal and non-Aboriginal people communicate. Mostly I hope for a better Australia where we can name the behaviours, thinking and positionings that diminish some to elevate the other, and where we no longer maintain a very unwise consumptive practice that causes extinctions and a weakened way of living for us all.

There is a Gudanji/Wakaja focus, which may or may not be heard, because that is my community, and had been the place of my research. More than that, though, it is my cultural reality. As a child, I grew within that community. I have what many people refer to as mixed heritage, but I did not grow with that part of my community who make it possible for others to claim I am not a real Aboriginal. I grew with Aboriginal people who practised Aboriginal ways of thinking, knowing, being and doing. Like everyone in the world, I am a product of my nurturing, my community and my heritage. Therefore, I am Gudanji/Wakaja and I must acknowledge that I have Kalkadoon heritage. Identity is more than skin colour or a quantity of melanin. As with those who identify simply as Australian and ignore the fact that their ancestors arrived here in very recent history – which makes it possible for them to also potentially be identified via such abhorrent terms as half-caste, octoroon or quadroon Australians – I identify in ways that honour my parents and their work in raising me without the worry of or attention to blood quantity or indeed skin colour.

The question of identity and the relationship to blood quantum is deeply problematic for Aboriginal Australians. For too many of us, our identity is judged by many outside our community according to the colour of our skin. The difference between me and people who deny me the right to identify in ways that are valid and appropriate for my community is this: my heritage comprises people with a range of skin colours that are not white or black alone. This is not a rejection of other communities and/or identities that may have been mine; it is simply who and how I have grown into becoming. It is not possible to reject something that was never mine and I certainly have no interest in becoming that which I am not.

As a Gudanji/Wakaja person, I have grown with a particular linguistic background, and it is not Standard Australian English (SAE). In my community, we had our language first and some people used some English vocabulary, in some contexts, to ensure they could participate in work activities. I highlight the change from SAE to English language vocabulary because it is an important part of understanding some of the motivations for writing this book. SAE, the formal iteration of English language here in Australia, is typically expected to be used in education, the media, law and politics, and is not necessarily used by all Australians as everyday speech.

I think it is imperative at this point to reflect on the occurrence of the English language here in Australia. English is an important language within the broader context of the global community, but it is in a deeply confronting location for colonised peoples. Its location for the coloniser also poses difficulties, if one was so inclined to ponder. It is not possible for a language that has evolved in one place, for one community of language speakers, to travel and operate well and with care, in a colonised community. Work must be done to ensure that language grows to encompass that new context and its new speakers in the fullness of their community. If that does not happen, I believe that colonisation is continuing, and that assimilation is continuing and that both of these are continuing to cause loss for those colonised populations. I claim this because languages grow for and about communities. They do not only contain the rules that tell us how languages work; there are many underlying and invisible contributors to languages that do not always articulate the ways of other places well.

As Gudanji/Wakaja, we now use English language vocabulary so that we can participate in school, and access such local community facilities as shops, social events and the picture theatre – *sometimes*, but that story is for another day. As children, we learned to read, to write and to speak English but through all of that we maintained traits of our first ways of communication, particularly non-verbal methods that govern meaning-making, those that operated, and continue to operate, in our homes, families and communities where we engaged with others just like us. Spoken language users make sounds, or utterances, to create words that are understood by others who operate and produce the same sound-utterance words. We make choices and decisions that are incredibly fast and invisible about what words we use and how we use them to make sense – it might be thought of as using a code to share messages with others who know and understand the same code. The greatest moral here is that every language community has its own distinct code through which sense-making happens.

Many ways of sense-making go hand in hand with those other more commonly known rules that we were taught at school for effective communication but there are other sense-making ways, hidden and often unknown. Indeed, those silent and invisible ways in which individuals across a community make sense may be the first component of communication and one that directs, in distinct ways, how and what we share as messages. This mostly unconscious practice is common to all children and, indeed, to adults. A key component in the effectiveness of our communication with one another is who stands at the front of the classroom or at the shop counter or at the ticket office of the picture theatre – it is dependent on the presence of those who speak the same language that you do. For members of the dominant English-speaking community in Australia, their communication and language use, in the fullest sense, will be affirmed and confirmed in all those places, and more, such as media, billboards, even street signs. Teachers have referred to this as environmental text. For Aboriginal Australians, however, our first languages are not SAE. Accepting this is important because languages do not grow alone and in isolation. Languages come with many necessary accompaniments and accoutrements that not only identify the need to learn but also what languages should be learned, and how.

People in my community speak English to varying degrees according, and in response, to their needs. I studied to become a teacher, so I speak a type of English which allows that work, and which is close to SAE, but is not the way I speak at home with family. My mum worked as a telephonist, so she spoke a different language from what was spoken in our home. My dad worked with cattle and, mostly, other Aboriginal men, so their language was different again. Languages have always been a tool to allow people to communicate with one another in ways that work for that purpose, and languages are always in a state of flux. Languages stretch and shrink, they grow, and they become thick and rich with the knowledge that is held by the communities in which they exist. They expand to include new behaviours and new entities in their communities while discarding the words that are no longer needed. Languages seem to me to fulfil such pragmatic functions, always carefully working to keep the sense-making ways that exist outside the words, but that occur to ensure the words can do their work.

This ever-evolving practice can be better understood through a study area called semiotics – which is simply the way communities identify, interpret and understand the signs and symbols around them. Semiotics allows us to understand the multiplicity of ways in which communities transfer knowledge within those same cultural groups but, more importantly, it also offers us ways to understand how other communities, different from our own, operate. I believe that a semiotic framing is at the very core of developing better and more considerate ways to communicate across the culturally different communities that Australia has always contained.

As explained above, languages are created by and evolve within communities for the needs of those communities. They reflect the values, the norms and the mores of their speakers and develop in response to their social, economic and linguistic requirements, or in other words, according to the cultures in which they operate. Vocabulary or spoken words are simply one component of a much bigger communication process. Communicating is significantly more nuanced than uttering sounds that produce meaningful words and it is impacted by many other considerations.

Although languages grow according to the needs of the community, they also have their own rules and laws. SAE has a set of grammars that standardise vocabulary use. We follow those conventions when we use a language because then we can be assured that we make sense and that we understand the messages shared with us within that specific community. Alongside grammar and punctuation, which show us how to arrange vocabulary, other important parts of languages include syntax, phonology, morphology, semantics and pragmatics. However, when multiple languages are being spoken within a geographic space, there must be another critically important addition to that list: semiotics.

It is essential to recognise that although several linguistically diverse communities may share a sign or a symbol, what is known of that sign or symbol within each community may, and is likely to, differ because all human communities have different ways of relating to one another and to their environment. I am convinced that understanding semiotic function from an Aboriginal perspective can add vital knowledge to how we, Aboriginal and non-Aboriginal Australians, interact and communicate in ways that respect the cultural identities and diversities of us all. In fact I believe that an understanding of semiotic contexts is necessary for all different cultural groups to engage respectfully with one another, whether Aboriginal and non-Aboriginal or not.

It is crucial to understand, too, that the way in which language or communication occurs in my community is as different as it is the same as SAE. The first Australian languages are not a deficient form of English nor are the first languages primitive or simplistic or unevolved. The first Australian languages do no more and no less than languages all around the world – they reflect and respond to the values, knowledge-making systems and understandings of relationships between entities within their community.

Many researchers claim that at least 250 languages and up to 800 dialects were spoken here before James Cook landed – before the arrival of English and its evolution into SAE. This density and diversity of language is commonly understood when considering the African, Asian or European continents, but not so much in the case of Australia. There is no single Aboriginal language. Aboriginal languages were, and remain, distinct from one another, with all their own unique and specific traits. The first populations spoke several languages and multiple dialects that supported trade and a range of other interactions with neighbouring groups. We were, and in some parts of Australia still are, speakers of many languages and dialects, and anywhere else in the world, those speakers of multiple languages would be celebrated as the polyglots they truly are. There is also that earlier mentioned trait of all languages, the invisible and tacit implication of how meaning is made and how communication exists in all its forms beyond utterance.

Aboriginal people lived, and many still do, in and with their environment in a way that would now be described as sustainable, but no single word could encompass the complexity of that existence. It is important and useful here to reflect on the longevity of Aboriginal occupation of this continent. Methods of living and organisation occurred in ways that demanded individuals work not to take away the rights of other human kin, or the rights of our non-human kin, but rather to support the wellbeing of all others. The careful and judicious use of resources, strict rules governing the harvesting of food, the range of travel across a given landscape and non-negotiable laws around the social organisation of peoples ensured an existence that was contained and stoic.

Australian languages grew and evolved to articulate and to perpetuate this way of living. These interdependent relationships between the human and non-human population are negotiated and acknowledged via vocabulary exchanges and constitute a key and significant difference in how languages evolved here and the language that now plays such a significant role in this place. In the simplest sense, the three participants in the way this communication occurs – human, non-human and utterance – all hold similar importance and share validity. There is, however, limited recognition or understanding of what this linguistic presence and diversity means in a broader context, and there is even more limited knowledge of what a semiotic focus offers to understanding what such practices bring to ways of communication. There is also another complication: the limited conduct of research from an Aboriginal perspective, which extends English language vocabulary that is cognisant of Aboriginal thinking. I will explain later why I suggest it is reasonable practice to extend English language vocabulary and not merely offer an Aboriginal interpretation.

This is important work and it brings together the philosophical traditions and definitions familiar to Aboriginal Australian communities and to communities far from Australia where English was birthed. These well-travelled traditions, also companions of and arrivals with that Whitby cat, have a different process of sense-making, one that, having grown a long way from here, still struggles to find its Australian land legs but one that now controls the discourse of our entire Australian family. The ways of sense-making that now live with Aboriginal thinking ways and English language vocabulary are making valiant attempts to allow old and new Australians to speak together but there are big gaps in that conversation.

* * *

Typically, linguists will identify the language practice, where I come from, as Kriol. This means that I and others who speak Kriol often use English vocabulary differently from people who speak SAE, or who have English as a first language. Linguists will often say that Kriol evolved as a survival language, one that developed quickly to facilitate communication between two different language groups.

In my community, it was to enable Aboriginal people across the top end of Australia – the Barkly Tablelands and into the Kimberley specifically – to work in the cattle industry.

Linguists also describe a language that has arisen out of mixing English and an Aboriginal language as Aboriginal English (AE). AE is a valid language with its own set of rules and grammars and is not, as is often claimed, a 'bastardised' form of English. Many have believed that Aboriginal folk are not educated enough to have a fuller grasp on the English language, but AE has evolved with its own set of rules that insist on a type of standardising that informs its use. Of course, as more research is conducted in this area of language use and cultural interactions, terminology changes and new knowledge is added.

I want to acknowledge, particularly, the contribution of many Aboriginal folk in numerous communities who, for a long time, have worked to maintain our languages. I also want to acknowledge other Aboriginal academics and researchers who are making important contributions to this knowledge because it is through their work that distinct practices in our ways can be seen and understood. My contribution here, hopefully, can help to stop the constant leak and loss of traits and practices that make Aboriginal cultures what they are. The work of non-Aboriginal researchers, too, is important, and has specifically made it possible to revive many languages, but it is vital that Aboriginal folk contribute to the understanding of meaning-making in Aboriginal languages. Because they live inside the environments that motivate language growth and use across the community, their insider knowledge allows important nuances to be revealed and told. To reflect Aboriginal thinking, a new vocabulary within the English language must be created, and it must not be merely translated ideas or knowledge. 'Lost in translation' is a reality when a dominant language group assumes the power or authority, even if it is unintended or kindly, to speak for a minority through the same ideas and concepts that exist for that dominant community.

The notion of in translation covers too many assumptions and has allowed important practices that have been instrumental for healthy Aboriginal living to become soft and passive. It has also enabled the vocabulary of SAE to be used in ways that do not contain necessary traits, ideas and ways of Aboriginal peoples. In response, and to moderate that loss, many of the common thoughts, values and/or knowledge held by non-Aboriginal folk are not explicitly reflected in this book. This is because it has Gudanji/Wakaja at its centre. It assumes the validity of Gudanji/Wakaja ways of thinking, knowing, being and doing. This is not a privileging of our ways; rather, it is the application of the same assumption of right that is made by the dominant community. It is in no way aggressive, or angry, just as much of the claiming by the mainstream Australian community is not aggressive, though there can, of course, be overt dominant behaviour because a large group, through numbers alone, can exert control and subsequently claim authority over others.

Different cultures occur because we are just that, different, and our differences grow in ways that are deeper than what we hear in utterances alone. Significantly, in the case of the First Australians, our differences, when measured against or articulated via English language vocabulary, will mostly be seen as deficient and the strengths and wisdom that have enabled the longevity of these civilisations will not be recognised. One example of an erroneous messaging about Aboriginal Australians is the often-applied word, 'nomadic'. This word, which means 'migratory' or 'moving from place to place', does not recognise the systematic and structured ways of travelling across a defined landscape. It does not represent the thinking, knowledge and disciplined decision-making that means people can relocate to another environment, one that has had time to regenerate since its last occupation.

Since Cook, Aboriginal Australian lives and ways of living have been defined through the vocabularies, the concepts and the perceptions of people and languages that are not our own. And unless the identification and articulation of Aboriginal ways of thinking, knowing, being, doing are at the beginning of discussions for and about us, too much is lost. I am seeking to offer a deeper explanation of how English and Aboriginal languages typically operate and the complexities that, as a nation, we still do not ponder. Sadly, this lack of consideration reverberates throughout the Australian community in ways that do not reflect well on any of us.

Some of the discomfort and anxiety that readers may experience can also arise because of an important national narrative, one that most Australians hold dear. As Australians, we pride ourselves on being the lucky country, on giving everyone a fair go and on treating everyone the same. Such beliefs may be important for national cohesion, but they contain falsehoods and rely on those assumptions of right. Australia is the lucky country only for some. A fair go has a different face when it is identified from a different perspective. We cannot treat everyone the same when not everyone started the same, when people come from distinct cultural heritages or practices. It is often assumed that the details of the human condition are universal and can be represented by Western articulated understandings and definitions. They cannot. Living within distinct communities and geographic spaces, and the ways in which social and spiritual connections are understood, mean that the details of the human condition are many and varied. It should not be assumed that such concepts and arrangements are a standard truth or that non-Western peoples aspire to the Western norm.

I want to introduce three significant concepts that play an important role in this conversation and that come from important Western theoretical traditions. I want to explore ways in which the dominant vocabulary can genuinely become more inclusive of others. I believe that, as a nation, we can stretch and expand our national vocabulary to truly move it from the distant northern hemisphere to its new location in this southern land. Words such as home or food, and of course there are many others, look very different for different cultures. This type of difference existing within understandings of a single word is called polysemy. Narratives can be, and are, told by a range of tellers, in ways that contribute to, participate in and share common stories. This multiplicity of voices in the telling of a story is called polyphony. And all narratives have multiple forms of their telling – through media and the voices of individuals, including other creative practice forms – which is called polyvalency. These three terms are critically important to what is contained in this book and will reappear later.

I am not advocating the sidelining of English language or SAE, but I am advocating for something more – the stretching and growing of English language vocabulary to include Aboriginal Australians and our more-than-ancient knowledges. It is becoming more and more critical that we begin growing ways of relating to this place through vocabulary that includes the new Australians and that reflects our unique and distinct place. Australia currently has a strange kind of thinking when it comes to humanity – a singular perspective. This place was never singular, but it was inclusive, and with some reflection on and awareness of both our own practice and the practice of others, we can return to that necessary component of the human condition.

You may not control all the events that happen to you, but you can decide not to be reduced by them.

Maya Angelou

Inventing fridges and wearing watches

While teaching at various tertiary institutions over the years, I have often been asked questions like this: 'Well, if Aboriginal people are so intelligent, why didn't you all invent the fridge?' And we can substitute for fridge, houses, telephones, watches, cars and various other inventions of the modern era. Those questions often ignore or are unaware that during the time that is being asked about, no one had watches or fridges. Most cultures, of course, had ways of cooling but not the specific modern, much-desired refrigerator. The stuck in the past, sedentary picture of Aboriginal Australians is a curious notion because those asking such questions have assumed their right to an evolving culture where living remains contemporary. Aboriginal Australians have also remained contemporary, and I imagine the rolling of eyes and the shaking of heads to show disappointment when the grandmothers of my grandmother heard her ceremony songs or watched her use the fighting stick in ways that were not traditional or failed to reflect their long-ago practice.

Recently I had a student who was working to record native animals in an important research project collecting population data. He felt it necessary to tell me that a particular marsupial, which built a specific, very visible type of environment for itself, was unknown to the people in that area and that those local people had not been able to tell him anything about that animal. He could not imagine that it would have been impossible for those living in that community not to have seen or known of that animal through their thousands of years of living in the same space. He could not imagine that he was simply not considered ready to receive the knowledge. He could not imagine the depth of lost knowledge because of his lack of or willingness to engage in respectful protocols.

Those questions about fridges and such, including knowledge of long-time co-habitants, have not generally been born of intended spitefulness but rather of genuine ignorance, though I also get plenty of that other kind too. My response is often as inane as the questions themselves because they are so very frustrating and too constant: 'Well, we didn't need a fridge' and sometimes, on particularly bad days, 'There wasn't a wall to plug it into.' Then the teacher in me kicks in and I respond with the faithfulness and heart that teachers have: 'We have always understood and practised a sustainable way of living where others, beyond the individual, human and non-human, were more significant. It was always against the law to take too much and accumulate. If someone did take too much outside of their share, there was a swift community-wide response to remind that person of the error in their thinking. We were neither a soft nor a tolerant nor an understanding people when big laws/lores were broken or when individuals forgot their responsibility to others and to our non-human kin.'

I then speak about the cultural iceberg and discuss how much is unseen, underwater as it were, and speak about the different ways of thinking, of living. I particularly identify the ways of meaning-making that are assumed to be standard and show that they are quite distinct, according to a range of culturally derived situations and circumstances. The posers of those questions, of course, are invariably struggling to understand the implications of intelligent and conscious living in what is often seen as an empty landscape inhabited by a simple people.

I have been concerned with and experienced what Martin Nakata, an Australian First Nations academic from Zenadh Kes, also known as the Torres Strait Islands group, calls the 'cultural interface' for much of my professional life and significant portions of my personal life. I expect that it would be the same for all members of minority groups. It is a difficult area because it is generally identified as political positioning, but I do not see that it is a political act to claim our own right to expression, to insist on our ways to define ourselves. Certainly, the ability to identify the bigger components of our human condition through our cognitive functioning is simply a human right.

The cultural interface is also at the heart of the clash between the ways of First Nations Australians and the ways of non-Aboriginal Australians that has continued since the 1770 moment when James Cook sighted and subsequently claimed our country. I think it became so much more complex with the 1835 proclamation by Governor Richard Bourke of terra nullius or no one's land, in response to John Batman's attempts to purchase land from the Wurundjeri in what is now known as Southern Victoria. That proclamation moved the acts of colonisation from the claiming and clearing of land to become a comment on the capacity of those first inhabitants and their ways of seeing and understanding that world, and it cemented a perception of the First Peoples.

That labelling immediately destroyed any opportunity for First Nations Australians to participate in the development of a truly Australian dialogue. Tragically, it abolished First Nations Australians' opportunity and ability to articulate our essential being through the relationships formed with, in, on and through our world. It positioned us as *other* in our own lands and meant that others, still, spoke for and about us in ways and with words and ideas that have not grown here. Worst of all, it offered to those new Australians the assumption of right to do what was done across the next centuries: their claiming, and *clearing*, of occupied lands and Countries that did in fact 'belong' with and to communities of peoples. It ensures, still, the supposition of our lack of complex living, in ways that were, and remain, structured and law-enforced, often stoic and self-sacrificing, but that also ensured the wellbeing of our non-human kin – what is now called sustainable and known to be highly desirable and important.

I have come to understand that the biggest untruth yet to be considered by this not so new country of Australia, is that we, the first occupiers, also have deep intellectual traditions that must be recognised in any attempt to engage respectfully, meaningfully and authentically. Terra nullius, and other words such as claiming, conquering, clearing, settling, civilising, invading and colonising, have created a narrative that has silenced and made invisible the knowledges that have grown and lived with this place for as long as we have done. Those same words have made it almost impossible for new Australians to be cognisant of other ways of thinking, knowing, being and doing beyond their own.

The inhabitants of this continent were not waiting to be explained and defined by the newly arrived. The civilisations of this place have been so long-lived because of the already existing knowledge that had grown and evolved in response to their needs and environments. First Nations Australians have never considered that our lands were unoccupied, uninhabited or unowned by either human or non-human entities. Indeed, the concept of ownership has long existed here and is merely one of those polysemic words. It simply has a very different face to how ownership is understood by those newly arrived. We have lived collectively in sustainable and deeply hospitable ways with the breadth and the breath of the entities around us, according to the relationships given through our kinship systems. Our practice of ownership is understood through the responsibilities we have to one another, to our non-human kin and to our Country – a non-individualist concept that places others first and that insists on careful moderation always.

Terra nullius was never the truth of this place, simply a convenient claiming by others to expedite the theft and the horrors which accompanied that taking.

Before and still

My parents made their children the focus of their lives. In their work, in where they chose to live and in their relationship, what was best for us was always a genuine and deep consideration. I also saw many other examples of this where I grew up, though that narrative is not one that is typically associated with Aboriginal families.

My mother often removed me from school and taught me herself what she feared I wasn't learning there. Those times remain my biggest learning moments. I became a student of the Brisbane Correspondence School (BCS), excitedly waiting for the bundle of books to arrive wherever we were located, mostly delivered by a small plane with a large letter 'B' on its tail. I don't know what that 'B' stood for, but it always caused my sisters to sing, 'Big B is coming, big B is coming.'

Mum taught me so much – understanding words,

making constructive attempts at pronunciation, building interesting sentences, reading many genres, mathematical principles, oh, and the mapping and penmanship lessons. I had marks on my hands a few times where the wooden ruler had slapped my fingers when I failed to map or write just so. I don't remember if the marks had come with pain, but my handwriting can be beautiful when I want it to be and my cartography skills are amazing.

I believe that, in those primary school years, Mum's teaching made the biggest difference to my learning because she and I shared a language practice but, more than that, a communication practice, a way of thinking and sense-making.

* * *

I completed my PhD in 2021 after ambling through study for what felt like much of my life. From when I started Western schooling as a child of about four, I just stayed with the learning – sometimes in schools, sometimes with my family and sometimes in my head – juxtaposing and entangling my community with the new one that has begun its growth here. I have been either studying or working 'in school' ever since, having graduated to become a teacher in the mid-1980s.

Eventually, my curiosity was further piqued by seeing how children in my classes learned and the relationship between what I needed to do to facilitate that process, how I adapted my behaviour to assist them in that journey and how they responded to my pedagogical methods. As a Gudanji educator, I noticed that what was ostensibly my instinctive practice, which worked well with my Aboriginal students, often needed to be made overtly different for my non-Aboriginal students.

It was getting to the end of the 1980s, a time of much change, and several years earlier, I had graduated from James Cook University of North Queensland. Despite the name, I had a great experience there and was privileged to learn with my student colleagues and from lecturers who engaged critically with knowledge and learning.

One of the most challenging moments of my time at James Cook was when the then Premier of Queensland, Joh Bjelke-Petersen, visited. His arrival coincided with the introduction of fees for tertiary study, though I can't recall if that was his motivation for coming. As the premier addressed the gathering a white male student standing beside me threw a flour bomb at Bjelke-Petersen and promptly ran away. Shocked by his action, I naively remained standing there. I understood the frustration of my fellow students, having attended several rallies to protest against the new system, and I neither liked nor appreciated the policies of that government and its leader, which made life for Aboriginal and Islander Australians difficult, but it confounded me that this student had assumed it was okay to do such a thing. Bjelke-Petersen turned and saw me standing there, raised his finger to point at me and said into the shocked silence, 'You! You're nothing but a half-smart, half-educated half-caste.' My then seventeen-year-old self was horrified and terrified by that reaction. Back then, I had heard one of his colleagues, a mining magnate from Western Australia, suggest putting something in the water to sterilise the half-castes because they were the ones who were the problem, the ones who caused the trouble.

About the same time, Mr K. Mabo, a student colleague better known as Eddie Koiki Mabo, was fighting for his country on Mer Island, and Professor Henry Reynolds, one of our lecturers, was publishing books that documented Aboriginal resistance and frontier violence in ways that recognised the wider implications of such engagements. I saw the non-Aboriginal community's response to Mr Mabo's fight and to Professor Reynolds' work. I can still see, in moments of reflection, the deeply disturbing and erroneous television and newspaper advertisements claiming that the 'Aboriginals were coming to take the backyards of hard-working non-Aboriginal folk', the subversive undertone suggesting that Indigenous people did not work, hard or otherwise, and were attempting to take something they had no right to claim. Both those men persevered. And I saw other people, my parents included, who persisted in working to achieve a better community. Surrounded by people who were quietly courageous, I decided that I liked Premier Bjelke-Petersen seeing me as a half-smart, half-educated half-caste. I liked it because it reminded him of the role that white Australians played in those awful times this country still struggles to claim as our national history, but it saddened me too because I imagined I saw a level of self-disgust there that must gnaw at something deep inside the human spirit.

In the mid- to late 1980s the education department in Queensland was moving through some big changes and had committed to integrating children with special needs into mainstream schools. This meant that schools were in various stages of responding to that process, cognisant of the complexity and of the need to support students, their parents and teachers. I was working as a school-based, then called remedial, teacher. Part of my role was to provide pedagogical support to teachers who now found themselves with special needs students in their classes.

In western Queensland, our school staff were gathered to start the new semester, as schools continue to do, with whole of school meetings to provide inductions, introductions, in-services, overviews and reflections. On day one, I presented myself to everyone as the remedial teacher and carefully handed out referral forms so my classroom-based colleagues could access my support. Our school had an enrolment of approximately 600 students, about 200 of whom were Aboriginal or Islander. That first day went well and on the morning of day two I walked into the staffroom to find my pigeonhole full – of nearly 200 referrals. Almost every Aboriginal or Islander student had been referred to me. I felt confused and devastated that my teaching colleagues believed that nearly all the Aboriginal and Islander students required learning support. Many of those students were known to me outside school – some were part of my immediate and extended family – so I knew that they did not have any specific learning needs. I wasn't sure what had motivated those referrals, but I was part of a supportive, skilled and knowledgeable team of education specialists, whose integrity I had to trust. I therefore decided I would treat those referrals as valid responses.

After consulting with several members of the specialist team, I conducted the assessments, which indeed revealed that many of those students did not need learning support. Further discussions with the vastly more experienced teaching and learning team of special education experts identified a need to develop teaching methods and strategies that responded to diverse learning requirements. And that need was not a result of anything more than cultural differences and an overarching lack of awareness about how cultures affect thinking and learning.

And then there was an incident in the first years of my teaching that continues to evoke my reflection. And no, I am not referring to the time my principal told me I was to teach that Captain Cook discovered Australia or face the possibility of being sacked, though that contributed additional inspiration, if I needed it, to do this work. As a new teacher, it had been suggested that I sit and observe a woman who had a reputation for teaching excellence. She was indeed a wonderful teacher but then I saw something that made me aware of the complexity of such a label, a polyvalent complexity. She sat with her year one pupils seated around her on a mat. The children were volunteering words that rhymed with 'pig', which would then contribute to a range of spelling lists she would prepare, aimed at each child's academic ability.

One little boy had a parent, recently arrived from overseas, who spoke English as a second language. He volunteered a word that was not recognisably English, but the teacher acknowledged his contribution and celebrated his courage to share it with the class. She said, 'Oh, I think that's a word from your mum's language. Let's write it up here and when she comes in this afternoon, maybe she'll tell us about this word, and she could perhaps help us spell it the right way.' All day that word held the attention of those students, written in coloured chalk on the top of the board at the front of the class with a cloud bubble around it to show its significance. All day the students watched that word and waited for the mother to come in to tell everyone about a new and different word. Spelling that day was fun and interesting and exciting.

But one student, that first little boy's friend, was

perhaps not so excited. Seeing the positive response to the offering of a word in the morning session, he took his turn and volunteered a word. The teacher's response disturbed me. She immediately, and with genuine kindness, assured the child that, 'Oh no. That's not a word, but it's great that you tried. Well done.' She promptly moved to the next child. That second little boy was Aboriginal and the word he volunteered was mig. Most Aboriginal people from many parts of Queensland would recognise that word as a shortened form of migaloo, a word from an Aboriginal language meaning white person. I hope that, in our contemporary Australia, migaloo is known to many people along the east coast of Australia. It is now a name given to a white whale that swims along the coast. Back then, however, as I explained the meaning of migaloo to that teacher after class, the breadth and the irony of her rejection was not lost on either of us, and she was horrified.

* * *

The notion of cultural differences was then viewed quite differently from how it is now. Ongoing educational and social research has uncovered many ways in which everyone can respond more appropriately to those who come from and with a culture different to their own. But as data from Closing the Gap, the Commonwealth, state and territory governments' strategy to address Aboriginal disparity, shows, despite significant spending on research and training, Aboriginal students are still experiencing poor outcomes, which continue to impact their adult lives. Too often, it is the students and their families who are blamed, either overtly or covertly, for these poor results. What if there is a different reason?

Teachers work incredibly hard at their job. Most do not enter that profession for the work conditions but rather for the joy of teaching and learning. Most are as passionate about their students' wellbeing and success as they are about the subjects they teach. I believe there are several complications to the teaching of children in the context of a post-colonial community and that a conversation about this is long overdue within Australia and has positive implications for both teachers and students.

I have worked in remote places and witnessed the hard work of my non-Aboriginal teaching colleagues as well as their struggle to accept the knowledge, advice and skill offered by their local Aboriginal teaching assistants. I have been told by non-Aboriginal colleagues that they have studied hard for four years to gain their knowledge so how can the local people, who do not speak SAE, be helpful? They fail to see that those local teachers already have more knowledge of the learning processes or mechanisms of the students because they share the same cognitive functioning, the same thinking ways – ways that do not currently sit with the theoretical explanations of non-Aboriginal educational theorists, which articulate the big, overarching or metanarrative that starts explanations from places of origins. I flag here that First Nations education theorists such as Professor Nakata, as well as Professor Karen Martin (Booran Mirraboopa) and Professor Lester-Irabinna Rigney, have contributed research that identifies the necessity of such work. Martin speaks about ways of knowing, being and doing specific to Aboriginal contexts; Rigney highlights the necessity for research conducted for, by and about Aboriginal contexts.

The pressure on those non-local teachers, often poorly prepared for the work that is expected of them, is real and weighty. My university work in pre-service teacher education has shown me a full and busy curriculum, just like that which exists in schools, and research conducted by Aboriginal researchers, through Aboriginal defined parameters, is happening but is still relatively limited. Sadly, providing deeper understandings of ways of knowing, being, doing and thinking, Aboriginal or otherwise, is still not a common teacher preparation topic.

Perhaps one of the contributing factors in need of closer consideration, and certainly broader thinking, is how the communicative process, in its multiple forms and functions beyond vocabulary alone, affects what we say and how we say it. In other words, how semiotic considerations impact meaning-making and understanding between two different cultural and cognitive traditions who are using approximately the same words or vocabulary.

Within Australia, the populations of its original inhabitants have experienced some of the biggest changes to long practised ways of living in an incredibly short span of time. Where we were once 100 per cent of the population of this continent, with successful societies that had lived in such ways through thousands of years, the activities of 'settlement' decimated families and communities almost to the point of obliteration. While it is understood that damage was done to spoken languages, the unseen and wider implications for communication in its fullest sense have not been considered. If peoples who have lived by and with a communicative tradition for thousands of years suddenly lose the use of that communication, without transition, the depth of the loss, beyond verbal languages, is massive and complex. The ways of understanding one another, the articulation of a place-based, grown way of engaging with the other living entities in that same shared environment, the ways of understanding practices and perpetuating the philosophical teachings – are all shattered. It is not by words alone that we communicate.

Because, in Australia in 2024, First Peoples comprise 4 per cent of the population, we are in the relatively precarious position of lacking real authority and economic power to direct our own lives. Having this control is not a rejection of the non-Aboriginal Australian culture nor is it a suggestion that Indigenous folk lack the ability to live with the paraphernalia of Western living. Rather, it is the need to simply be who and how we are.

The viewing of this continent as a 'bare' landscape, showing no signs of occupation that were recognisable to the British, and the thinking encompassed in that, has contributed, and still does, in my imagining, to the negative positioning of Aboriginal peoples. As a teacher, I have witnessed many times when good, hard-working colleagues have made judgements about Aboriginal children that were based on such ignorance. Through neither spite nor hostility, but simply a lack of knowing of how Aboriginal Australians' living practices have evolved across thousands of years, the relegation of Aboriginal contexts is swift and has become a natural response from too many other Australians.

I remain confused and disturbed by this positioning of Aboriginal cultures/people because I cannot see these same groups in the adverse context in which they are typically placed. What I do see are the results of poor and underdeveloped knowledge, opportunities, experiences and expectations of Aboriginal people by too many members of the new Australian community. Mostly I see a language system that has grown for and about a non-Aboriginal community a long way from this place, a language that needs help to evolve into its new environment. There is, however, an unfair burden on teachers with overfull curricula and limited, if any, university-provided opportunity to learn about those deep cultural differences in ways that are defined and explained by those from the diverse identities and heritages that now constitute Aboriginal populations. There is even less work on the overt expanding of the shared vocabulary of SAE that would position and suggest alternative views to the possibilities offered through the long-evolved knowledges of Aboriginal communities.

When my own children started to be framed by that negative thinking as they went through school, the imperative to teach them myself, and then to conduct a specific type of work and, subsequently, research to produce a different knowledge, became even more urgent.

New opinions are always suspected, and usually opposed, without any other reason but because they are not already common.

John Locke

Old places and their yarning

In my research, I was motivated by the need to identify the very rich, storied knowledge that continues to be embedded within and dependent on living with our Country. This relationship and connection to Country is well known to Aboriginal peoples but many of the details of how those connections develop, evolve and are maintained have faded into some nondescript space that offers neither hint nor clue of the complexity of the deep cultural knowledge, its structures and systems. This has arisen through the assumptions of colonialism and events tenanted in such upheaval, including the loss of Aboriginal peoples' own languages. Any assumption of sameness in the recognition of signs and symbols, and how they are perceived by communities, will cause too many misunderstandings and too many losses for one group, and too many untruths for the other. The extreme difference in how old and new Australians relate to the physical environment can be considered through a time lens. With real or lived knowledge of the interdependence of people and place, the fostering of careful relationships and ways of being within the presence of the non-human have garnered a particular human behaviour and form. And it is one that newer Australians struggle to comprehend and/or replicate or perhaps even be truly concerned with.

The ways in which people, place, flora, fauna and weather phenomena all engage and become entangled in one another's lives form a profound and deep-seated connection that grows and evolves through long occupation/practice. Knowing that resources were not in perpetual supply necessitated judicious living by everyone – even in good times. I do not simplify the difficulty in enacting a good and rewarding life. Many times I have walked all day to gather enough food, food that I was entitled to consume, so I have a sense of the reality of the physical endeavours, and an understanding of the pitfalls in harvesting too much in one place. Yes, sustainable is a good description of Aboriginal ways of living, but it does not include the layering of the spiritual, the lores and the laws which add extra dimensions to that sensible and conscious existence.

It did not occur to me that to be concerned about signs and symbols was a significant jump. I, too, had assumed we, Aboriginal and non-Aboriginal Australians, had a sense of clarity about one another's cultural contexts, but then I started to learn about Western traditions and realised I had missed so much of what was unique and distinct for both groups. Civilisations had existed here through a careful and disciplined reading of those signs and symbols and lived well because of that – just as has happened in communities throughout the world. We, Gudanji and Wakaja, know what constitutes signs and symbols and we are taught by our community what they mean, and how to read them, and we have always been successful learners. Without that success, we, and many other first communities, would not have survived as we have. Since 1788, however, when the First Fleet arrived, new systems of constructing meaning have been growing, and while it is assumed that Aboriginal lives have been improved by those, I remain unconvinced. These imposed new signs do not always fit comfortably. I think Aboriginal Australians try to make them fit, but our bodies and our brains remember the first ways that continue to ensure we remain who we are.

When it came to studying for my PhD, I thought that for this to be 'valid', it must be a theoretical exploration of the topic/question – researched, researched and then researched some more. And my notion of research was a very traditional Western one. I would develop a question, pose a theory, gather data and analyse it. And I believed that, as academia expected, I absolutely must not insert myself into the research. But then I realised something that caused me to pause, to change direction and conduct the study through practice-led research methods and not those traditional methods.

I saw that this expectation of no self in the research came about because the research was typically being conducted by someone for whom academia had evolved – a Western self. In other words, traditional research paradigms and methodologies were created by, with and for those in the dominant community, with supporting research produced by others in the dominant community, in the language of the dominant community and analysed through theoretical concepts and definitions, yes, again, from the dominant community, of which academia was also part – the Western self was already present in all its forms and reiterations.

Those from a non-Western language or community do not experience the privilege inherent in that because their cultural constructs cannot easily or comfortably be contained in Western definitions and their philosophical underpinnings cannot be adequately articulated by Western vocabularies alone. And although there is nothing inherently wrong with what academia expects, it must recognise and accept that there are deep differences in ways of thinking, knowing, being and doing, ways of making meaning, which all depend on cultural constructs, that they are in no way deficient or less, and that they are as valid as Western ideas, traditions and ways.

I came to understand that I could create the same academic space for myself that was assumed in more traditional research practices. I could utilise the philosophical underpinnings of my community; I could utilise the linguistic traits and characteristics of my language, while using the vocabulary of SAE. With some stretching and pushing and fertilising of the English vocabulary, it was possible to speak an alternative, but as valid, truth that worked for who and with what I know from my community. I had to follow a different research path because my *self* is not a Western self, and I believed there was the real danger of me perpetuating those same gaps in understanding the fullness of Aboriginal knowledge if I did not extend the boundaries to claim my Gudanji context.

I did, though, fear the process and what would be required to conduct what was, for me, an ostensibly new and frightening method of study. Just as the quote, 'Those who can, do; those who can't, teach', is typically uttered by people who lack the knowledge and skills to teach, the creative process for knowledge production is more complicated and exacting than it appears. I had never truly considered myself to be creative, able to articulate otherness as a new centre – that was the work of the great thinkers and artists – but such an approach would allow me the ability and freedom to write through and with the thinking that I had grown with and borne witness to as I flourished in my community, always with the presence of my parents, my family and my Country.

The place where I had grown, in all its facets, was not the wider Australian community, it was my own cultural space, the space where I later took my own children for them to grow into the bodies that they have inherited, and to learn the knowledge that comes with those bodies. In our Gudanji/Wakaja community, I saw them grow into confident, happy people, with skills and competencies that have enabled them to be contributing members of *all* their communities, because I am not entirely convinced that we as Aboriginal folk (Gudanji/Wakaja people) live in two worlds. To my way of thinking, the concept of two worlds allows a continuation of two separate dialogues and no expectation of developing an inclusive Australian narrative encompassing all its human and non-human record.

There is an important pedagogical method called Two Ways Learning, which is most typically implemented in remote schools where there is a significant population of Aboriginal students. This practice, which highlights the need to understand and operate through both Aboriginal and non-Aboriginal ways of teaching and learning, is not what I am alluding to when I state my distrust of walking in two worlds.

Terraglossia, not terra nullius

There is no result to be found if you Google the term 'terraglossia', and you won't find it in a dictionary – yet, and perhaps not ever. It is a word I have coined because in making the untruth visible, populating the 'great Australian silence' with the sounds that have been yarning here for thousands of years, we must identify the words that illustrate or define Aboriginal and Islander ways of thinking, knowing, being, doing and seeing as defined by us through our concepts, and not merely non-Aboriginal concepts massaged into something that is close enough. In the context of living terraglossia, it is Country that becomes the ancient and modern academy, the teacher and the sage and the mother, where knowledge sits waiting to be seen, understood, felt and heard, ready to be taught and learned, and then used as we need it. It is also the recognition and the acceptance of the more-than-human and the kin arrangements of interdependence through which all entities live within and share the occupied space. Terra nullius does not explain this place; terraglossia starts to by the simple reminder that we do not exist alone and that what we do as a privileged species, we do to us all.

'Ngurruwani Gudanji-marndi maga guda gurijba iligirra gamamjani' – Gudanji come from the hills and fresh water. This statement in my language signals polysemic and polyvalent ways of imagining self beyond its location in a geographic landscape. We do not live without Country. Gudanji often see geographic or weather phenomena as stories, and therefore we expect to hear, we listen for, we think about, we feel and we remember voices shared through, in, on and with the hills and the fresh water. As we listen for those voices, we expect and wait for them to contribute to our own personal and other human voices, but we also have a responsibility to (re)present those voices that are beyond human utterance, to ensure they are acknowledged and heard. And this way of belonging can be better articulated through the term terraglossia.

Later Australians' lack of knowledge of and resulting inability to read and hear the voices in our Countryscape enables the terra nullius claim but does not make it true. The ignorance of our storying methods does not negate their existence nor their roles in the lived experiences of Aboriginal peoples. The claim also highlights how far those new knowledge systems have travelled and their inability to respond fully to their new context, something that is becoming more urgent in the climate emergency due to the destruction of landscape and extreme levels of species extinction on this land.

I also coined the term terraglossia specifically to clarify and flag my non-appropriation but precise claiming of SAE and its associated linguistic traditions. If SAE had been offered as a choice, perhaps, the occasional comments from speakers of English suggesting my appropriation of this newer language might be valid. But SAE has been forced upon the Aboriginal community. My privilege means I have developed a level of competence in SAE and can utilise it to engage with a certain section of my wider community.

The use of Latin to create the term terraglossia was also a deliberate act. In its simplest form, terraglossia means tongues of the earth or earth speak. In a fuller reading or understanding, terraglossia can be defined as the non-human utterances that occur within a cultural Country and the provision of knowledge to those who hear those soundscapes and understand them to contain messages/narratives about living with the earth and all entities. Latin is often regarded as the language of scholarship, and it, too, has a deeper tradition and use across the world. By deliberately framing a Gudanji philosophical practice in this way, the notion of terraglossia cannot have its meaning lost in translation or appropriated. Most importantly, it is more difficult to put aside and be identified as Aboriginal business that does not involve the wider non-Aboriginal Australian community – that claim that allows and accepts the non-responsibility of some of the Australian population to learn about its truer and extended history and people. It is also a response to my living in my world, which comprises a diverse range of languages and cultural spaces beyond the human, and which intersects with the culture of the West.

Australians are all aware of the arrival of the First Fleet, though this seems to be something of a contradiction, since Western knowledge claims, even insists, that Aboriginal Australians had arrived here *first* via some form of seaworthy vessel (not a fleet) thousands of years before. Can you see what has happened in that claiming? Can you hear, beyond the words, the discarding of everything already located here on this land? A polysemic repositioning, a polyphonic relocating as *other*, in a paradigm that sees everything since Cook as the standard, the norm. Can you imagine the breadth of the polyvalent marginalising and the suppressing of more-than-ancient knowledges in all its modes, practices, categories and themes by a culture newly Australian and in a language barely out of its infancy? A language that has grown in another place, for another people, which travelled here in 1770, surely cannot be expected to be sufficient to articulate more than 60,000 years of the evolution and development of Aboriginal ways.

* * *

This place has always been home to a multiplicity of distinct civilisations, their cultures and partnering languages and practices, grown here with the first populations' work in adapting to a variety of landscapes. The newly arrived Australian culture landed here in the very recent past with its own set of practices and mores. As a new nation we are perhaps only now beginning to grapple with the complexity of our shared history. Human structures do not and cannot house the knowledge that has grown across Aboriginal communities because Indigenous knowledge is constructed in bigger and deeper ways than can be stored in books alone. Indeed, it continues to live and evolve beyond and despite the human, and our seeming unrelenting need to control and manipulate the physical environment for our own purposes as if the land were a playground for the entertainment of children. It occurs to me that a more considered examination of why a penal colony was established here on 26 January 1788 is also essential and perhaps a decent thing to do.

As a new family of Australians, federated since 1901, our beginnings are glossed over and almost always viewed through the impact on Aboriginal Australians, and I do not disagree that this was almost beyond bearing. I wonder, however, what conversations we could have if we spoke of what effect those beginnings had on the human cargo of the First Fleet and those other ships that brought convicts here for the next 80 years, and how that affected the way in which Aboriginal and these new Australians engaged with one another. People convicted of seemingly petty crimes, unable to be 'housed' in the overflowing hulks anchored in the Thames, were transported to Australia. Many were young people, but most, I expect, were part of families. What is the mental damage and what is the physical response to such treatment? Claiming and building a 'home', even in a landscape that was beyond foreign, was surely a priority. I imagine that negotiating with people so very unfamiliar was not.

Many years ago, Professor Rhonda Craven, a non-Aboriginal academic with extensive experience in the tertiary sector, suggested that history looks different when you're looking from the shore rather than the ship. History looks different when it has been entrenched within place for thousands of generations, when living has always been about the care and maintenance of others, both human and non-human, learned through those historical teachings. Daily living, too, looks different when it has emerged in entangled but also structured and formal manifestations of the human/non-human relationship. Our Gudanji histories demanded an individualistic engagement and responsibility to a collective living where resources are not accumulated by a single person or group, but what of the histories made by those expelled from their homelands to a place almost unimaginable? Perhaps new Australians can truly leave the ship if they plant their feet on the shore to live better with this place.

Many a telling story

I grew up with kujiga – Gudanji and Wakaja soul – with Gudanji kujiga travelling with the Mararabarna songline.

I was Pbirrianjulunga first, so I am Gudanji, but I am also Wakaja. We are the people of the northern and south-eastern Barkly Tableland respectively in the Northern Territory of Australia – two distinct peoples. Gudanji understand that our big kin, our Country, encompasses vast plains, hill country, rocky gorges, fresh water and other living entities. Being from such diverse landscapes, we have developed and practised, and continue to develop and practise, ways to live and learn through a multiplicity of communicative forms.

My knowing of and about my Gudanji and Wakaja self does not grow from carefully filtered and then repositioned knowledge, shared with me by someone outside my cultural context; it comes from lived experience and knowledge shared with me by others who also live the knowledge and who share the same kinship bonds. This lived knowledge ensures the continuation of Gudanji and Wakaja in vast cultural Countryscapes and has safeguarded our maintenance of more-than-ancient occupation with, on, in and through Country.

I am also Kalkadoon. My mum's father was Kalkadoon, but I do not feel Kalkadoon in the same ways that I know myself to be Gudanji/Wakaja. I grew on Kalkadoon Country and spent important growing time with my great-grandfather, who was also Kalkadoon, and who taught me some of the language, stories and histories, but I still struggle to feel Kalkadoon. Slowly, I am becoming a better daughter of the Kalkadoon.

I do not live in two worlds – I tried that and then realised, as mentioned earlier, that this allowed my newer Australian family to continue not participating in the learning required to live well within this landscape and not improving their understanding of the philosophical pillars of Aboriginal Australians as they are described in our ways and words. I see the convenience in being able to separate Aboriginal and non-Aboriginal communities, but this separation perpetuates the tensions and lack of ability to be cognisant of alternative ways. The insistence on two worlds gives new Australians the opportunity to tell me what I should aspire to, to *become* more acceptable – ignoring the fact that I am who I am, and neither need nor am able to become someone else.

As a child, I lived in remote places with few distractions beyond family and what entertainment we could create and access together. There was the physical environment – and we had books. We lived on the edges of Wakaja Country. My mum is a descendant of both Wakaja and Kalkadoon, and my dad, Gudanji by blood, went through Wakaja ceremonies as a young man due to colonial events: his mother, her siblings and their father left Gudanji Country to escape a massacre. This arrangement of parental identity history and formation, described in terms such as descent and blood and ceremony, has not only affected and informed how I see myself as a Gudanji and Wakaja woman but also how I have learned about relationships between my Country and me.

My dad grew with family on Country, practising a culture that predated the Western arrival. His family eventually lived alongside the new arrivals who claimed Wakaja and Gudanji country to establish vast pastoral properties. They kept a careful separation – two communities where contact was often marked by violent and destructive clashes. My mum grew in a different context and while her identity as Aboriginal is as valid as my father's, realistically her lived experience could not contain any of the older cultural practices in the overt ways practised by my father's family. Her context meant it was important to live in ways that ran parallel to non-Aboriginal living, to engage with some practices that evolved into new ways of identity and being. Her family gained an uneasy, insecure peace with the inclusion of Western cultural norms, but the impact of those inclusions is deep and tormenting.

Because of the complexity of the recent colonial past, the changes experienced by so many Aboriginal peoples have been too fast and too consuming and too often couched in terms of loss and a lessening of our sense of ourselves as Gudanji or Wakaja or any of the other hundreds of first civilisations in this place. I have heard our contemporary cultures referred to as hybrid, as if other cultures can change and evolve and still be whole, just not us. Significantly, with such notions of hybridity to describe identity and cultures, a barrier is set, as if those two separate worlds are real. More importantly, the notion of hybridity seems to suggest that there is a 'pure' example in the first instance. I cannot and do not live a life that is separate; the contemporary living is mine and all the attendant artefacts that have come to this place are mine also and like others who claim and define themselves through the first ways, not blood quantum, I am still Gudanji, Wakaja and becoming Kalkadoon.

* * *

As a BCS student, I read books. The stories were of faraway places, told in a language I struggled to feel, about people

I struggled to understand, and those story words were just black marks on a white background that didn't nurture me with any embedded wisdom. I read those marks that barely made any sound in my ears. I saw them and ascribed meaning to them as they sat silent on those pages. I couldn't hear them well enough to transpose them into my greater thinking.

I lived for the outside-of-school time when I was with my father. With Dad, I left those book words behind on their pages. Those fascinating but unfamiliar people and stories faded until my head was filled with voices speaking in tongues that I heard and felt deeply, and that did not make my ears do all the work of listening, my eyes do all the work of seeing. Stories with Dad often left me with ephemeral impressions so vague that I didn't know if they were memory scraps or profound living, happening in that very moment, or perhaps a beautiful gifting of both.

As I journeyed through BCS lessons, delivered by the diligence of my mother, come flood, fire, drought or plague – and they all came – those stories from books gave me the opportunity to know about other places and spaces that were not yet inherently mine. The books and their underlying narrative delivered me knowledge that was distant and second-hand, and that I could only partly appreciate. I could read black marks on a white page, I could even read the meaning of those marks, but I continued to struggle to *feel* the stories within those words as I felt the stories shared with me by my family, beyond those books. Those stories, and the ways I made sense in and of my lived world, were starkly different to what existed either in books or, later, in my school experience with teachers other than my mother.

I lived well and I lived close and intimately with the place where my family lived and worked. I stayed at school, left Country, became a teacher and, despite being highly functional in SAE, I continued to be perplexed by the ever-secret nuances in those new stories. My ongoing struggle to understand what lived inside those stories reflected my fragmented relationship with them. I was no longer just struggling with black marks on a white page; now I was struggling with words, their images and sounds, coming into my ears where there was nothing for them to hold onto within my head, neither inside nor outside of my body nor in my lived experience.

My struggle to amalgamate the book words with those external experiences would finally come to a head many years later. As a young mum I took my children home, to allow them to learn the lessons I had learned with my dad because I saw them struggle to be truly comfortable in their skin when we were away from family and community and Country. While we walked with the aunties, our Elders, who tenderly but firmly schooled my children, a sense of clarity came to me about the different ways in which my books (because they have become mine), and Gudanji and

Wakaja kujiga, both indulge us with their own distinct ways of meaning-making. I saw that our stories, informed by the past, are always busy with gifting us the present through the making of kin, as they prepare us to make and live a 'kinned' future.

As I have already mentioned, our newly arrived human kin would call this sustainable living, but this phrase does not contain the very necessary knowledge of how to sustain relationships to truly do this well. The stories from Gudanji and Wakaja are always occupied with making kin between us, all the entities and our Country, reminding us that we do not occur alone, that we are not separate and single, that we have an obligation to and must live reciprocal lives – this is the responsibility that comes of being human. I had returned home to realise that I had failed to find ways of making kin with those other stories and places, that, in them, I only existed alone.

I needed to remind myself and my children of our ways of relationality, both for their sake and for their ability to contribute to our community. Back in the 1980s, when I attended teachers' college, I and my student colleagues had been told that we had to teach Aboriginal children, specifically, how to make choices and decisions for themselves – individually. It was important, we were reminded, because Aboriginal children struggled to aspire to a future and struggled to set aims and plans that would allow them to achieve it.

From the early 1960s through to the 1970s, Albert Bandura, a Canadian–American social psychologist, had proposed what has become known as the social learning theory, which was studied when I was doing my teacher training. The theory suggested that it was through observation, imitation and modelling that children learned and acquired new knowledge and behaviours. These were important because they would allow children to develop as individuals with the right to plan and develop their own ambitions and lives. Aboriginal children, of course, had been learning through observation, imitation and modelling for generations and generations. What Bandura and other researchers whose work posed new ways for Aboriginal children's learning had failed to understand was that, for them, living in communities, as we did and continue to do, such individualism did not respect the interdependence of life. Living in isolation for 60,000 years in small distinct groups, where survival depended on others, meant that notions of collectivist living made sense. It is easy to be concerned for others when there exists a relationship that is imbued with mutual responsibility. Bandura's research did not appear to appreciate such ways of living.

Secret English

As a result of colonisation, the diverse populations of First Nations peoples before the First Fleet are now even more diverse. We live in urban communities, seemingly little engaged with the practices through which we lived before 1770; we live in remote communities where SAE is a second, third or fourth language; and we live at all places in between. Our diversity, however, has several very real and salient points of commonality arising from recent acts of colonisation.

The first is our ongoing relationship with our Countries and our ongoing identities according to our Country. The next significant commonality, from my perspective, is the ever-deepening impact of Western ways on our knowledge systems. Although we have never ceded our Countries, nor traded them for a seemingly better life, a Western life, we continue to struggle to regain access to our lands, which newer Australians refuse to acknowledge as stolen. And they fail to understand how our relationship with Country impacts our wellbeing. These tensions about Country are more often represented in the media now that others understand the importance of and urgency for better and more sustainable relationships with the environment and its entities. A critical note, though, and one still not attended to, is this: Aboriginal bodies have evolved in our place for a very long time and therefore they require, to be healthy, the foodstuffs that grow in the locations where we have evolved. Why should that be so hard to grasp when we know that gum leaves do not make for a nutrient-rich diet for polar bears? Our lands are still valued for the resources they contain and their contribution to an economic success, not for the life-giving possibilities they represent, and certainly not for the wellbeing, the human rights, of Aboriginal folk or our non-human kin. The extreme abuse of so-called natural resources is being indulged in at such a rate that huge tracts of once fertile and life-sustaining lands now lie barren.

The third point of commonality also needs to be exposed: the critical and insidious action of sometimes overt, sometimes covert, but mostly casual, methods of silencing First Australians' knowledge and making it invisible. This is often, but not always, conducted through kind and gentle practices, with neither ill will nor malice, but the outcome is the same.

I worked once with a non-Aboriginal teaching colleague who was from a non-English-speaking European ancestry. I entered her classroom and found her shaking a small child and saying most aggressively, 'You will not speak that gobbledygook in my classroom.' The child, five years old, had spoken their own Aboriginal language. At that same time, we had a minister for education who was denying Aboriginal children the right to speak their language in the early part of the school day. In my almost forty years of working in a range of educational institutions and contexts throughout much of Australia, I have never once, by connotation or by explicit statement, heard anyone voice disquiet about English-speaking children speaking their own language in the classroom. Indeed, research shows that children learn best if they learn in their first language. This is not rocket science but it sustains a terra nullius thinking.

The violence of that one instance is absolutely not common, but the same cannot be said for the ignorance and the disregarding of the need for large concepts of the human condition to be articulated from an Aboriginal perspective. The violence contained in other methods of silencing Aboriginal humanity – and the making invisible of our ways – is wider ranging and surely as damaging. A number of years ago, I was the only Aboriginal educator on a team of seven conducting a review of the literature concerning research into Aboriginal education. One of the articles considered for inclusion in the literature review was a paper with a title along the lines of, 'We have told you this before…', which had been written by a team of Aboriginal educators with a diversity of experience and knowledge. Most of my colleagues did not think it was appropriate to include this paper in the project because they did not recognise any of the authors named in the work and those authors were not recognised academic researchers in that field.

Despite my insistence that it was entirely appropriate, indeed, necessary, I had to 'pull the race card' to get that paper included. My years of practical experience in Aboriginal education, the breadth of that experience – greater than that of anyone else on the team – my lived reality as both an Aboriginal learner and an Aboriginal teacher and my formal qualifications (at that stage, I had four tertiary qualifications), did not grant me any credibility in that situation. That I was forced to indulge in the equivalent of a tantrum showed me the lack of respect for the work conducted by the authors of that paper and reinforced the frequent claim by Aboriginal Australians that we are one of the most researched groups in the world, often as the objects of study and rarely as the contributors. For me as a professional, it suggested that I was the token, the one included to show the legitimacy of the project. It showed me, sadly, that the group was more concerned with the articulation of research from a specific perspective and that there was a perception, controlled by those within academia, about what was valid and what was not. I could not see that there was genuine interest in what the literature review might uncover and the new learning to be offered, certainly not if the knowledge came from Aboriginal experts outside the community occupied by those researchers.

One of the most tactless acts of cruelty, and perhaps it is better named racism, must surely be the sublimation of the more than 60,000 years of Gudanji/Wakaja first ways of thinking, knowing, being and doing. A key factor in my original research was the oral traditions of Gudanji. Languages, or linguistic forms, are critical to the continuity of cultures and their communities of people, but languages do not speak on their own; they need the companionship of other linguistic mechanisms to ensure that communication occurs. Although many of us learned some of the components of language at desks in school, it is not common to look beyond grammar, punctuation, syntax and so on. We don't often look deeper to consider semiotic implications through which communication is achieved. Only limited work has been done in exploring how semiotics – the reading of signs and symbols in and by a given community – differs between various language traditions and practices. Certainly, only a few Aboriginal researchers are doing the important work of defining such concepts through ideas and notions derived within

Aboriginal contexts, but our numbers are growing. This is not a criticism, merely a recognition of the current situation and the reality of being 4 per cent of the Australian population. This is concerning because semiotics may be one of the ways in which we can better understand cognitive and cultural impacts on the communication between Aboriginal and non-Aboriginal communities, and differences between English-speaking and non-English-speaking communities. It may also be one of the ways we can stop the ongoing leak of our more-than-ancient knowledge.

It is okay to ignore semiotics a little in a monolingual community, where everyone shares roughly the same communication processes, contexts and vocabulary, but semiotics cannot be ignored in multicultural communities. It must surely be a significant consideration if the wider community is to genuinely engage in deeper thinking appropriate for the twenty-first century. I believe that we require a serious exploration of the mechanics of how the basic signs and symbols of a community are understood and how meaning is construed through them. It must be understood that non-verbal meaning-making does not occur in the same ways across different linguistic systems and communities, and that theoretical concepts defined by one culture cannot stand for and encapsulate those in other cultures. And when those communities have been colonised, and the expectation is that all people speak English, it becomes even more urgent.

* * *

Throughout my life, in my various roles as an educator and when speaking with Aboriginal people, including work colleagues, from remote, rural and urban contexts, I have often been asked to explain discussions in meetings – what questions were really being asked – and to clarify what the non-Aboriginal person was saying. Indeed, I was often also asking myself and my colleagues the same questions. There were times when Aboriginal colleagues would say, 'But didn't I just say that?' in response to a non-Aboriginal person making a comment after moments of good and constructive discussion. These enquiries came from very clever people who were working in many different roles and had developed an extensive array of knowledge and skills. They were competent speakers of SAE and key members of their communities.

Then, in about the fifth year of my teaching career, I saw a quote pinned to an office wall that was attributed to an Aboriginal man in Bain who has conducted much research in Australia. I have tried to find the quote but have only been able to find research conducted by the respected Australian linguist Professor Michael Christie referring to 'secret English'. The quote said: 'We want our children to learn. Not the English you teach them but your secret English. To us you seem to say one thing and do another. That's the English we want our children to learn.'

I had not often been as excited by something on a wall as I was to read that note. It was even more exciting than the time, as a first-year student at teachers' college, that I went into the toilets. On the back of the toilet door, someone had written, 'I know God and she is Black.' That statement resonated with me and I wanted to share it with my mum. I rang her that evening and told her what I had learned that day. She told me to not go to that toilet again and that she had not sent me to university to read the backs of toilet doors. I tried to tell her there was a lot of writing there. She simply said, 'For the sake of God, close your eyes, Debra.' I had forgotten that we were in fact Methodist along with Gudanji and Wakaja.

But I had experienced that secret English as a learner, when I had truly been able to focus on learning with my mother without the need to be thinking about translation as I did with my other teachers. Now, as a teacher, here it was again in my classrooms and then it presented itself at meetings with non-Aboriginal colleagues. There seemed to be secrets everywhere. The complexity of this secret English grew further when I became conscious of the number of times I would happily stand in front of my class and ask the students to take out the story we had produced the day before. Non-Aboriginal students would produce the required work, but Aboriginal students would pause, just for a few seconds, before they followed suit. Often someone would say, 'Oh, I thought we wrote an essay yesterday' and when I reflected, I recalled that we had indeed written an essay and not the story I was now requesting.

I wondered what was happening and why it was happening so often, because I had done the things a good teacher does. I had taught literacy lessons explaining new ideas and concepts and I had certainly developed word lists with those classes which said that story, essay, composition, writing and narrative were different names for similar things, and we had learned those lists. And, when I listened to my own children and taught them in my classrooms, I saw the same things happening with them, and my casual curiosity turned to much deeper consideration. This caused me to revisit my ways of learning on Country with my dad in those open-air classrooms, and the methods used by my mum in the same places, and to ask why I learned so deeply with Dad and so differently with Mum.

As a child, I was a successful student and my ability to learn was sound. During the years of my mum's teaching, I averaged 97 per cent achievement rates, not because I was a particularly gifted learner or that my mum accepted less than best efforts, but for other more intricate reasons. First and foremost, Mum and I shared those deep sense-making ways beyond spoken language, and I could focus on the business of learning. Another important consideration in my achievement was my mother who, as a user of SAE as a second language, spoke it literally in the truest sense and not as many speakers of English do when it is their first language, through connotation. For her, as a teacher, if I did not achieve 100 per cent, it meant that she was not teaching as she should have been, and that, as a learner, I was missing important knowledge. Mum adjusted her methods to match my needs as a learner. There are considerations beyond this, of course, around the transference of knowledge learned in a literal way but that is not what I want to cover here. I can say that the antics of my sister did add the equivalent of at least four other students to the small class of BCS pupils Mum supervised/taught because, like me, my sister wanted to be outside but, unlike me, she was not in the least curious about those people in the books we read. My mum also supervised two non-Aboriginal children, and their achievement rates were high too.

It is much more complex than that, of course. It was also that my parents not only gave me the tools, on my terms, to achieve, but that they both had high expectations of me. At no point did they ever, in the words of First Nations researcher and educator Chris Sarra, 'collude with mediocrity'. And despite those achievement rates with my mum, the teacher who was and remains the most demanding of them all, I was placed in every remedial class when I went into town for high school because the school administrative team noted where I had come from – a remote place with my very young mum supervising me. Then one day in year nine my maths teacher said, 'You're truly bored in here, aren't you?' I didn't respond with more than a half-smile because I had been enjoying the nearly two years of reading time at the back of the general mathematics class. I was moved into advanced mathematics the next day and into other advanced classes – no more reading time.

So, my work and life experience has led me to be concerned with how Aboriginal people make meaning when using SAE. I pondered then why it was possible for me to know, deeply and surely, the messages, wisdom and learning from my dad and to consider what happened when I then moved to SAE. What was that secret English and how could I learn that clandestine way of meaning-making well enough to mitigate its impact in my classrooms, for my students?

The biggest consideration here lies in the organisation of the languages themselves. English is a binary language and Aboriginal languages are not. I touch on this later.

Not being WEIRD

As participants in the contemporary Australian population, Gudanji are restrained from many of what we consider basic rights. We are not able to describe the violent encounters we have lived through, and often continue to experience, with words such as invasion, slavery, theft, rape, horror, trauma and violation. Those words make our shared Australian history unpalatable for those who have not lived it or those who do not acknowledge as close a relationship with their ancestors as Aboriginal Australians. Our repositories of theoretical knowledge have been relocated into the singular categories of art and design because our new Australian family lacks the capacity to read the equivalent of our books or to understand our ways of meaning-making that also exist in our design work. Our oral traditions are not understood in the way that our Elders have used and continue to use them, so these strategic and intensely vital orations have become storytelling, myths and legends, and folklore.

Australians generally, and certainly educators, must consider the unspeakable, the secret and the silent. We must look for the invisible approaches that are not present in the need to erect monuments and impose control over the environment in ways that separate and categorise unwisely, that cause that classification of terra nullius to be applied beyond that 1835 labelling. For me, I can see that the assumption of terra nullius has been spread over Aboriginal communities as if it were a Harry Potter invisibility cloak. The supremely successful civilisations who, because of strategic and organised life practices governed through philosophical underpinnings, and not fate, have lived well for at least, as Western science tells us, 60,000 years. How do we consider and authentically explore what is now causing the relocation of those same peoples to occupy the place of poorest achievements, outlooks and outcomes?

Culture-based cognitive differences between the First Australians and non-Aboriginal Australians may account for some of these results. As Belinda Liddell, research fellow and deputy director of the Refugee Trauma and Recovery Program in the School of Psychology at the University of New South Wales in Sydney, points out, non-Western cultures practise a form of collectivism. They see themselves as 'interdependent with others', placing 'high value on social harmony, interpersonal connections and a holistic style of thinking'. Such cultures, says Liddell, are more interconnected with the physical environment and more dependent on context than those from individualistic Western cultures. She subsequently notes that research participants, including those who conduct the research, are typically from 12 per cent of diverse communities or from the self-named '"WEIRD" group – which stands for Western, Educated, Industrialised, Rich and Democratic'. This means that a considerable proportion of culturally diverse communities are not being represented or articulated in significant volumes of research.

If Western researchers do not systematically critique their methods and analytical practices, the burden is on Aboriginal researchers to identify alternatives to 'WEIRD' research, and some First Nations Australian academics have contributed seminal works on this issue. Many international First Nations scholars, too, have produced, and continue to produce, substantial works. The burden for Western researchers is to recognise that alternative truths exist. It is also important that they involve themselves in the use of such research in ways that recognise and do not appropriate the work. Then separation can be minimalised and the deeper knowledges of difference can be addressed to help facilitate a more inclusive discourse. A community can be built where First Peoples knowledge systems are understood to exist, to be valid and to be utilised to create kinder and more inclusive places. This, of course, requires the dominant community to accept that Aboriginal Australians know what is best for us; it requires a suspension of the notion of Australia as the lucky country, where everyone is treated the same. Mostly, it requires those from the dominant Australian culture to know that these requirements are not a rejection of Western thought but rather a need for a simple truth: that Aboriginal peoples not only have the right to be but also possess deep knowledge that can make good and necessary contributions to the wider Australian community.

Rather than merely establishing a distinct and separate Indigenous model, researchers need to have an inclusive, critical and reflective conversation. When they work with Aboriginal people, they must suspend their own thinking in order to accept other approaches and, as these are shared, not to translate them into standard Western thinking, language and understandings. Difference is normal, but it is wrong to assume that we all aspire to sameness. When wider Australian research truly includes and acknowledges our ways, articulated through our neologisms, our definitions and our thinking, then a more genuine awareness of Aboriginal knowledge will begin, allowing Aboriginal peoples to be part of the newer Australian community and conversation. Not doing this risks continuing to banish us again to the margins, while others define, control, allow and validate our knowledge systems in non-Aboriginal ways.

For example, in more recent times, the non-Aboriginal community has, as it should, started talking about their own contexts that include such words as culture, connection, tribe and other terms that have typically been part of the vocabulary explaining or referring to Indigenous communities. It is long overdue that the non-Aboriginal community see their living through these terms, but there is a danger inherent in this too. If our national conversation is not clear about the detailed differences that exist between Western notions and the meaning of those same terms within the Indigenous communities, those communities will again be marginalised, silenced and made invisible. There will, again, be an assumption of sameness, that Aboriginal and Western communities practise such concepts in the same ways.

* * *

During my own long study journey in universities, I was always struck, in my reading, by the thinking of some that Aboriginal people were not enough, not as civilised as the West, were needy and naive. Apparently, we needed to be educated into Western ways because we lacked those deep complex theoretical perspectives. It didn't sit comfortably with me that the *real* Aboriginal populations were still being considered through the lens of the uncontaminated noble savage, albeit in a more modern imagining, and many others of us were no more than troublesome half-smart, half-educated half-castes. It did not seem to me that savagery was more present in an unclothed state, and having lived and grown in the places I did, knowing the histories of family who had survived there, I knew that savagery existed in other ways too.

Mangaluwe - to talk

In Gudanji language, mangaluwe is to talk. To talk is everything but talking does not include just utterance and it requires a particular decorum otherwise we risk, as my dad always said, making the air stink with effluent. My dad was a straight speaker, so yes, it was a different word that he actually used.

Because my foundations are Gudanji and Wakaja, they frame the SAE vocabulary that I use, and that is used by those I talked to during my research. This means that, generally, there will be slight differences in meaning, but in some instances the Gudanji meaning will be quite different from the conventional SAE meaning. It is vital to understand that this reflects regional and culturally derived language changes, not poor use of SAE. A common example of this is the use of the word shame. Its meaning is distinct from what is understood in the conventional SAE usage.

Many of the people I spoke to use the vocabulary of SAE, but in ways that layer that vocabulary over Gudanji ways of thinking, knowing, being and doing. As well as enabling the continuation of Gudanji practice, these ways also ensure that Gudanji can articulate a response to the pervasive surveillance that results from being defined by and through the discourse of others, and particularly the insistence of the West on our conforming to the new Australian language. Again, I do not reject Western ways or language; I merely identify the lack of proper fit for Gudanji and possibly other First Peoples and acknowledge the work of First Peoples to make that fit better.

Since colonisation there has been an intertwining of Gudanji vocabulary with SAE. My research grappled with this duality and the signs, symbols and signals that are beyond interpretation and untranslatable – that, to be told, require new articulations. We have grown with our kin in ways that can never be fully identified as stereotypical archetypes or assumed to be totally encompassed in such statements as a literal SAE rendering of 'the land is our mother' or through that other word, connection. This kind of concept loses and simplifies the layered complexities and assumes a basic, almost ephemeral metaphor for birthing that does not begin to reach the depths of our relationship with our Country.

Too many Aboriginal people, including some Gudanji/ Wakaja, have lost the details of what exists through, and makes possible, our claim of connection. I do not wish to cause harm, merely to affirm there are a multiplicity of ways in which Aboriginal people understand their contemporary connection, as is our right. I do highlight, though, that through the strategic ways in which members of my family have survived and the subterranean lives they and many others have lived, my ways of connection are more aligned with pre-Cook practices of relationality.

Typically, where Gudanji people or speakers have been research participants, words are translated to fit into a predefined Western paradigm. I am not questioning the validity of those research projects. Indeed, for the work conducted by any number of linguists particularly, I am grateful. It is their work that provides knowledge critical to Aboriginal people's ability to regain some of what language has been lost through invasion and colonisation. It is a complex dance through the eucalyptus to make new steps that can navigate the Australian landscape and not just stumble through prickly spinifex clumps. We must massage definitions to suit and fully represent distinct Indigenous cultures, and the creation and contribution of new vocabulary, such as terraglossia, within our new language can certainly contribute to this.

* * *

In 2012, First Nations Australian educators and researchers Professors Mark Rose and Kay Price spoke about the longevity of Aboriginal occupation of this continent. Rose suggested considering a clock face and reimagining each of its 60 minutes as representing 1000 years. In conjunction with my graphic designer daughter, I have taken that thinking and developed the diagram below.

The outer circle shows the 60,000 years of Aboriginal occupation of this continent. Although much research accepts 65,000 years, for my purposes here, 60,000 is used. And to facilitate the reach of this illustration, I am focusing on Western researchers' ideas of 60,000 and not Gudanji knowing, from the times of Buwarraja, that indeed, we have grown here.

The next circle identifies 13,000 years, which is the extreme limits of what geographic researchers Patrick Nunn and Nicholas Reid claimed in 2016 to be the length of time that is possible for Aboriginal oral history to stretch back and recount a central 'truth'. To establish this, Nunn and Reid explored sites around the Australian coastline and listened to open stories told by the Aboriginal people living there. The researchers then compared those stories, which told of significant climatic and environmental events, with the geographic records held within soils.

The next circle, marking 5000 years, identifies when the pyramids were built by what we refer to as ancient Egyptian culture, and it is followed by the marking of 3000 years showing ancient Greek cultures, which have contributed many of the philosophical and theoretical underpinnings still influencing modern cultures and certainly the ideas imposed through and because of colonisation.

The next circle identifies the writing of the *Canterbury Tales* by Geoffrey Chaucer 700 years ago. This important piece of literature is generally accepted as the beginnings of what we now know as the English language. The shading in the final circle marks the arrival of Cook on the Australian landmass.

What are accepted as ancient cultures, the genesis of modern English and Cook's landing are all very young compared with that outer circle. Indeed, if 5000 years is ancient, is it not obvious that this word is not nearly enough to describe Aboriginal living with our lands for more than 60,000 years? And if modern English had its start 700 years ago, how can we imagine it is enough to define, articulate or explain the complex ways of knowing, being, doing and thinking that have enabled Aboriginal communities to live here so well for so long? On this clock, the longevity of First Nations Australians' occupation across our continent is as stark as Rose suggested it was. Why is it, then, that many in academia and the mainstream Australian population struggle with its validity?

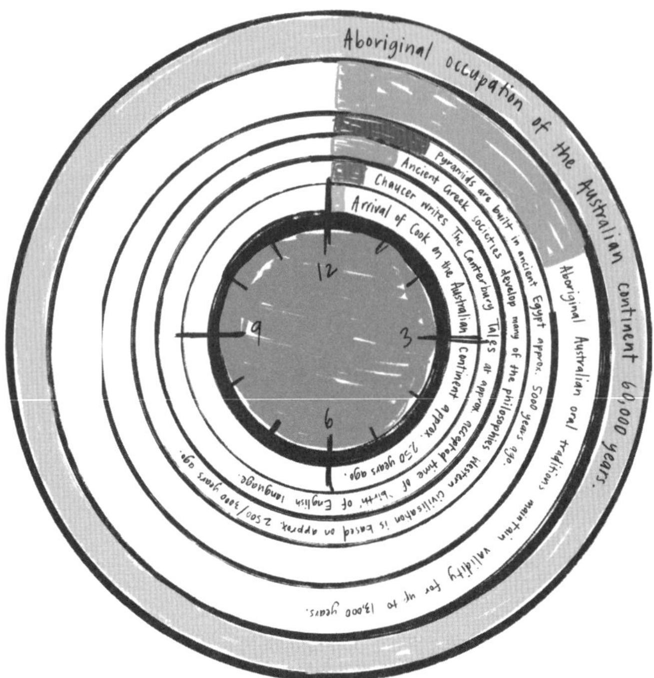

Representation of the last 60,000 years of human history.
©nardurna/Dank 2025

Gudanji and Wakaja ways

As a Gudanji person and, I expect, like too many other Aboriginal Australians, through colonisation and mainstream education practices, I have been systematically moved further and further from much of the cultural context that allows me to speak my ancestor language fluently. Colonisation means that I primarily speak with the vocabulary of SAE but, despite that, I use and understand those words in different ways, ways that remain secret and tacit, derived through meaning-making methods initially learned while growing and learning within my community, my family and, sometimes, on Country. I later learned, and now employ, the vocabulary of SAE in my daily and work life, and like books, SAE has become my language too, but my understanding and ways of meaning-making are born of Gudanji and Wakaja being. For all peoples, First Nations or otherwise, our engagement with our families and our communities gives us the methods and practices through which we begin to know our world.

Through acts ranging from anti-colonialism to desperate survival, Gudanji, like most other First Peoples, have adopted the vocabulary of SAE and incorporated it into our everyday speech practices while maintaining our more-than-ancient narrative ways that are sometimes overt and sometimes fugitive – overt and conscious practices such as maintaining and reviving of our own languages, and the fugitive, unconscious way in which the signs across our community are understood and used to create the meaning of our human condition. Through that process of adoption, I insert those new words into the Gudanji and Wakaja ways of understanding with which I relate to the world, the ways that reflect my Gudanji thinking, the ways that make this new world a kinder and gentler place through it becoming familiar.

I return now to polysemy, polyphony and polyvalency, those three important terms introduced earlier, because they are worth spending time with and they point to the different, as well as the same, ways people talk about our worlds. Polysemy generally refers to multiple possible meanings for a word. For example, when I hear the word home, I 'see' my Country as a geographic landscape populated with both human and non-human entities, the stories they tell through the utterances they each deliver and the laws through which I relate to all of those entities, including the history stories. My home is where my ancestor beings created Country in the time of Buwarraja and then the entities that share it. My home is not four walls, rooms and a roof. When my non-First Nations colleagues hear home, they are likely to see such a built structure, a house where their family has lived, which holds memories of people and activities. Our ideas of home are the same but ultimately very different. If our nation is to become a safe, healthy and nurturing place for all its inhabitants, we must reconcile those different meanings.

The same differences occur through many other SAE words such as culture, connection and tribe, which reflect constructs based on cultural values and which, when used interchangeably, miss the immutability of Aboriginal connection with our Country. Without clear articulation of the formal ways in which those concepts contribute meaning and make sense for each cultural group, and the formulation of new vocabulary that represents those unique and distinct differences, the dominant group controls the breadth and scope of meaning in our conversations. This, again, marginalises important meanings that exist within the minority group.

Polyphony simply means many voices and for Gudanji, these voices include the utterances of our non-human kin and of the geographic landscape. These multiple sound productions are seen as ways of communicating or telling stories beyond the human. When we understand that we do not live a singular and non-connected life, the sounds around us are as important as the sounds produced by humans. For Gudanji, hearing the polyphonic voices means the recognition of others within our living landscapes. Our connections are not through feelings, deep or otherwise, for these other animals. The connections are through real and long evolved rules and laws that identify who, what and where our individual responsibilities lie. Our connection, among other things, causes us to be responsible for the wellbeing of our non-human kin, to represent their presence and to act in ways that ensure the maintenance of their healthy populations and their habitat. Gudanji are born into these connections through our skin or kinship groups. We do not get to select or choose who of our non-human kin we represent, and if by chance I want to eat a particular animal species that it is against the law for me to eat, then I do not eat it. It is my personal obligation and responsibility to uphold that law, which always supersedes my personal rights.

Polyvalent means many forms. Here it refers to many forms of narrative as reflected in the many voices of both the human and non-human as well as the phenomena of the geographic space, including types of weather. Polyvalent narrative for Gudanji means we listen for and expect messages from a wide range of narrators, and we respond appropriately. As a child, I was with one of my older aunts when I saw a snake. When I got home and told Dad about the snake, my aunt said she had not seen it. I knew that she had because she grabbed my arm and pulled me away from where the snake was lying. She told me we were to go in a different direction and as I heard her tell Dad she hadn't seen it, I saw a look that passed between them that I later understood was a silent and tacit communication. Through that transitory look, she confirmed with Dad that there had been a snake, but her different connection to the snake meant that it was against the law for her to articulate its presence.

While I was living and growing on Country, sharing narratives and experiences with family, I heard language in diverse contexts, modes and forms. The movement and interactions of vocabulary, voice, experience and entities, and their created dimensions in meaning and sense-making, built my ways of thinking, knowing, being and doing, but included constants within the geographic landscape. The Gudanji hills and fresh water remain and continue to hold those formal memory records beyond reminiscence. They are stable reminders or referents of our narrative past, as well as giving opportunities and obligations to link our contemporary selves into that past through our ways of proper relationality. Those sites signal deep and long-held reminders of our responsibilities and our obligations and affirm the way our Country takes care and provides us with a good, if somewhat stoic, living.

It is this way of relationality that allowed Nunn and

Reid to identify that the oral traditions of Aboriginal communities maintained validity for up to 13,000 years. The sharing of encounters and occurrences calls forth an experiential relationship with past family, including non-human kin, formed through relationship and kinship obligations across the wider Gudanji landscape. The voiced collective sits in Country and is threaded through contemporary experiences as the Elders talk our youth and young people into the verbal landscape in ways that repopulate and recall Ancestor narratives of that collective past with the collective present. This polyphonic and polyvalent narrative form ties contemporary Gudanji people into our past and reminds us of our responsibilities and the obligations we have to ensure a future for all our kin, human and otherwise.

Listing to the more-than-voices

Flora and fauna, as well as geographic forms, weather and phenomena, are all part of a mutual interdependent living. For Gudanji, and I'm sure, for other Aboriginal Australians, such living reminds us that what we do to the animals, plants, land and climate – our non-human kin – when we fail to heed our kinship responsibilities, they will ultimately do to us. The communication systems used by Gudanji have the flexibility and depth to cohesively support, encourage and attend to those non-human voices and their messages. Those voices may be heard through the songs of birds and the yelps of dingos, but they are also heard in the rustling of leaves and in the night-time scratchings of animals. Voices exist, too, in the noiseless bubbles rising from the turtles or fishes in the waters and in the smells on the wind.

Australian linguist Rachael Nordlinger, the author of *A Grammar of Wambaya*, and others, have conducted research to form a body of work representing parts of Gudanji language through Western notions of linguistics. Her work, which comprises crucial vocabulary lists, and explanations of grammar and pragmatics, has been and remains essential to Gudanji's ability to retrieve some of what was lost through the trauma and horrors of invasion and colonisation. As Gudanji and scholar, I remain respectful and forever grateful to Professor Nordlinger and others for their commitment and care in producing their work. I believe that we as a nation are now ready to truly understand the breadth of communication in and of Aboriginal contexts. We must use insider knowing, together with linguistics work in areas of Aboriginal Australian languages, to become fully cognisant of the impact of 60,000 years of linguistic evolution.

Gudanji, through the articulation of four genders – male, female, vegetable and neutral – identify and recognise the presence of others beyond humans. This recognition of 'otherness' emphasises the need for further exploration of semiotics in relation to Gudanji, by Gudanji, with insider knowledge, to identify and articulate what remains tacit and therefore more easily unacknowledged or obscured in non-Gudanji framings. This is important work because Western language theorists and semioticians have identified binary manifestations in English language and suggested that concepts exist in pairs: male and female, black and white and so on. They generally suggest that meaning is made through the relationship a concept has with its opposite; for example, good is good because it is not bad. In the arts, villains are dark and heroes are light, in character or dress or both. This concept is particularly strong in traditional children's literature, for example, *Snow White*, *Beauty and the Beast* and others.

Gudanji language operates differently, through a system that can recognise and respond to relationships. As with its multiple gender choices, this kind of system provides for multiple ways of engagement of and by the participants in the communication process. As with mankujba, words can have multiple meanings and the participants in the exchange must make choices in how meaning is made – according to formal, systematic and structured relationships.

* * *

For Western semioticians, the amalgamation of the idea of something (signified – idea of a crocodile), the sound or image associated with that concept or idea (signifier – sound produced when the word 'crocodile' is spoken) and the final meaningful unit (sign – vision of the crocodile sitting on the riverbank) is the widely accepted way in which sense and meaning are made. For Gudanji, however, the act of meaning-making is also contingent on relationship. Lived experience, along with knowledge drawn through shared narrative events or accounts from previous generations who are in a kinship relationship with the listener, provides a critical checking mechanism for the meaning-making process.

Relationships affect the ways in which meaning is made within our countryscape. Community members will participate in and with, or *ignore*, narrative events according to their relationships. As with the interaction with my aunt and the snake, during my research, and indeed, during my living as Gudanji, I observed that, although a group of people might all see a weather event or other phenomenon, its meaning would be filtered through relationship rules and laws and then explained and told from various viewpoints, thus producing a range of similar but different narratives constructed from that single but multiple perspective. So, when several Gudanji are simultaneously experiencing a strong breeze, for some the breeze may be bringing message clouds, for some the breeze may be telling that there is no fishing today and for others the breeze will be in partnership with other contributors to narrative, such as the rain or coming sorry business.

A young woman who had worked with crocodiles, and had many stories of her interactions with them, recounted seeing the ripples on the water. Indeed, she was expecting them to appear after feeling a slight breeze. Drawing forth her lived experience and the knowledge derived through being on Country, her relationship with her grandmother, both formal Gudanji kinship and the biological relationship, and the experience of crocodile hunting shared with her grandmother, she listened to an inner narrative to guide her in a highly dangerous situation.

Other Gudanji who have lived and grown in the same context as this woman will have different narrative-formulating relationships and thus different ways of *being* in that same moment. A young man was asked to return to camp to collect matches. When they reached the agreed fishing site, the other group members were shocked to find that he had already collected the matches and was sitting by a fire with fish caught and ready to cook. The group comprised both siblings (biological and kinship), who had a shared upbringing and many shared life experiences, and non-Gudanji visitors, but the siblings, too, were surprised at the speed of his trip.

When asked how he managed this, he replied, 'My feet know this place.' The siblings shared smiles and unobtrusive nods while the non-Gudanji visitors asked, 'Oh, so you ran fast along another track?' Although he had used an alternative track, his words expressed several other meanings. Gudanji insiders heard a non-verbal, tacit expression of relationship existing between feet and place, almost altering a more typically temporal logic of speed and distance, inducing a deeper knowing, which in turn effected a swifter journey. Gudanji also heard affirmation of ongoing, multigenerational living where feet have had multiple reiterations through cyclic life journeys – the long-lived experience of feet. It was accepted and recognised that *feet* can have their own knowledge as a distinct entity, and that the young man represented the 'voice' or 'authority' of the feet. In his words, the feet were ascribed knowledge through their continuous walk with, on, in and through countryscape, including with the young man's predecessors or antecedents. The shared Gudanji understanding of his words was reflected in the neutral gender status, which recognised the beingness of feet and the reiterations of a specific set of feet throughout Gudanji history as distinct entities with identities separate from, but connected to, the bodies to which they were attached.

Another young woman danced with her family and was able to reimagine the long and significant number of women ancestors dancing with her. For her, the voice of the contemporary singer acted in a way that bridged the past and the present so that she understood herself to be dancing in the presence of those ancient Gudanji women. This reminded her of the responsibility she has to maintain the connection with people and place to ensure a future dance ground with those yet to come.

Such comments are not romanticised or poetic expressions, or magical, ephemeral thinking but part of a worldview that recognises the validity and agency of distinct and separate entities and reflects a non-hierarchical existence, in which the inclusion of all other entities is expected, demanded and honoured.

Although many Gudanji now typically use the vocabulary of SAE, our ways of meaning-making do not always follow recognised grammatical and pragmatic practices as understood by the West but appear to 'sit over the top' of ancient Gudanji linguistic practices. This results in the multiplicity of understandings of the comment, 'My feet know this place.'

* * *

And vocabulary is not always the most significant method in the communication process. In the early days of my marriage, my non-Aboriginal husband and my father sat out the back of my family home during Dad's lunch break. In earlier conversations it had been decided that we would go fishing and camp out bush for the coming long weekend, and my husband had volunteered to organise the trip and pack. I watched as my dad, now rushing to return to work, proceeded to communicate with my husband, in typical Gudanji-style chat, about what he should pack for the trip and where to find those items. On later reflection, I came to understand that there had been many hand motions and several words that to a non-Gudanji might appear somewhat random, all interspersed with the typical silences, almost imperceptible head motions and facial gestures familiar to old Gudanji and Wakaja.

When Dad left to return to work, my husband went to the shed and proceeded to collect a few camping things. When I asked him what he was doing, that those were not what Dad had identified to be packed, but that he had said he wanted these things, my husband replied that my father hadn't said anything so he was packing as best he could. I said that of course Dad had told us what to pack and proceeded to list all the items. With my husband still insisting those words had not been spoken, I realised he was right. Dad had communicated in our ways because he was in a hurry to return to work and had slipped into the most comfortable, familiar and natural form of narrative, and it was not what my husband was familiar with.

Respecting relationships

Stories link generations from the past, through the present and into the future. They then become methods of storing knowledge; relationship or kinship becomes the key or the 'code' to unlock the contained knowledge. Story and knowledge are plaited together through relationships that require reverence, tacit understandings and patience to establish and cultivate; they cannot be extracted and set to use without the appropriate accompanying context.

The role of Country is essential. Country holds the elements of past events through geographic formations but also holds more personal mnemonics that trigger recall and remind people of more individually relevant acts of significance. For example, let's consider a tree that grows by the cliff face – perhaps where an uncle was born. Shade from the cliff, the soft earth produced through the composting leaf matter from the trees, the angle of the sun as it hits the rock face, creating warmth but not heat, the level of privacy afforded by the placement of the tree and the cliff, and the proximity of medicinal plants all combine to provide a good place for childbirth with attributes similar to a hospital. Decisions about appropriate childbirth places can often be made generations before but are extended into contemporary contexts according to the combined conditions and the story events understood by people.

The welcome to the child given by soft earth, the gentle heat of the warming rock and provision of medicines, if needed, and the protection given all establish a relationship with both child and mother. This lasts for the life of the child but is also verbally related to the next generation as a special place that has given life and so is part of a formal awareness of reciprocity in distinct family contexts. Both the child and the mother maintain their own unique narrative with that place and in a relationship that goes beyond the birth link.

Ways of knowing the touch of the breeze, the warmth of the sun, the smell of the earth and water, continue to build connections between the human entities and the non-human but ever-living landscape. These deep relationships maintain the connections that have changed the casual landscape into one that becomes intimately known.

Gudanji are never alone on our Country. We walk in extended moments of silence to listen for those non-human, non-sounded voices through mankujba. Our ability to maintain cultural continuity, including oral traditions and social practices, depends on our ability to remain 'entangled' with our place and kin. I have watched my children, not only those who I have birthed but all my Gudanji children, grow and walk on Country. I have watched their feet touch the earth in almost soundless steps as they walk with deep consciousness of the earth. I have seen them listen and engage with those kin who are differently voiced and who are not mobile in the ways of humanity – as we must do to live well as Gudanji people.

For Gudanji, ascribing titles and names to what are now identified as geographic forms assigns relationship and creates a distinct mode of relationship-building and *knowing*. Such recognition moves entities from inert geographic features into *being*. Entities referred to as geographic forms in Western thinking are kin for Gudanji. They cause us to always be conscious of our past while *living* in that unique, unrepeatable moment as an unbroken thread of continuity.

Through deliberate performance and ceremony, Gudanji entities, including humans but by no means limited to them, are intimately connected with one another. In the course of my work, I documented the reciprocal relationship that exists between human and animal kin.

During the collection of food, specifically the conkerberries that Gudanji and the bush turkey both enjoy, the Elders accompanying the children recounted past acts of berry collection. Through the awareness of mutual dependence – humans and turkeys – but also their interdependence, I could see the notion of an entangled story, eating berries, human kinship arrangements and human consumption of the turkey. I once watched a documentary in which a non-Aboriginal person, insistent on understanding where their food came from, visited a butcher shop to appreciate the process from the bullock in the paddock to the steak on a plate. It was a critical moment for that person but the separation between them and the bullock did not offer them the fullest learning of the importance of interrelationship and the layered messiness and real accountability involved in the taking of a life. Their experience had been sanitised by visiting a butcher to view an already lifeless carcass.

And the two distinct stories are linked when the turkey is consumed by those for whom this bird is a food source. These people observe the collection and the consumption of turkeys with the view to protect or even perhaps respond like the jungai – those who are responsible for safeguarding the laws and ensuring that they are followed during ceremonies. Jungai notice the number of turkeys being collected and who is collecting them from which part of Country. This knowledge may result in the turkeys being collected from another place or in the forgoing of collecting for a time. When there is little rain, and a lack of the grasses and berries typically consumed by the turkeys, humankind will not collect turkeys for food and will choose to consume something else. Thus the voiced and mobile (human) membership of Gudanji community ensures the observation of laws of sustainability and the future protection of the community. Gudanji practise a stoic existence, making choices based on what is best for the whole community into the future and not living an immediate, indulgent moment that rewards individualist thinking.

The messages from the turkey can be read through its presence on Country. The turkey involves itself in the narrative of kinship and place through its presence at gathering places. It is also articulating its story of kinship when it consumes food items that are shared with human populations. For turkeys, the conkerberries are an intrinsic link with their human kin, illustrated by both the sharing of the food source and the shared enjoyment of it. Gudanji rush to the places where the conkerberries grow but we always make sure not to take more than we can consume in the same day – this is law and not a random act of altruistic concern. By regulating our practice and consumption, we ensure the turkey has enough to eat; we also illustrate our willingness to share resources and in that way to continue the life kinship.

The understanding that this current experience is not new, unique or singular removes the ambiguity of personal and group politics and populates the cultural landscape with memories used to remember the living events within Gudanji place. Place expands to include past places, where narratives sit and are stored until they are recounted again. Human entities then have the freedom of personal experience, but Country holds the grand design.

Kin and skin

Our engagement with Country and with kin is governed by understandings of relationships and how they work. The first way I *am* in the Gudanji community is through my father Lurick or, to give him his bush name, Thodia. I am Pbirrianjulunga; I am also a direct descendant of Limbijari, my great-great-grandfather. His son, my great-grandfather, is Wundigarrangunu, and my grandmother is also Pbirrianjulunga. These names give me ways of relating to Country and they give me ways of being Gudanji within the context of a *biological* family. They also allow other Gudanji people to know how I am connected to them. These names place me within a landscape of Gudanji antecedents and allow my presence to be located within that landscape by people from those groups who are part of our extended kinship systems such as, but not limited to, the Wakaja, Garawa, Mara and Yanyuwa peoples.

These names offer a small part of the detail of *how* I am Gudanji.

Importantly, names are attributed according to birth, birth order and relationship with names of antecedents. I am Pbirrianjulunga because it was my grandmother's name, and I am her eldest granddaughter. Pbirrianjulunga is also the name of my eldest granddaughter.

Overlapping our personal names is the next level of relationship; skin names are categories within our kinship system. I am Nimarama skin. My skin group relates me to others who are external to biological relationships but just as important. In many instances, skin family connections are as significant as biological ones. Nimarama gives me my extended family, but not in the way this is understood in non-Aboriginal vocabulary and social constructs. Skin associations come with significant expectations.

Gudanji are born into skin groups according to parents. It is important that the lines linking parents and offspring are maintained since this ensures what is referred to as 'straight skin'. Being straight skin means there is clarity concerning the rules governing social and ethical obligations, responsibilities and reciprocal relationships, not purity of blood. Thus, for me to be Nimarama, my mum must be Niwanama and my father Jurulaku. My daughters are Nulanyma, and my son is Jukudayi. Significantly, when I took my non-Aboriginal husband-to-be home, family immediately placed him within the appropriate skin group to ensure their grandchildren were straight skin. Therefore, my husband is Balyarrinji. This diagram shows Gudanji skin groups.

Husband	Wife	Son	Daughter
Jiyanaku	Nurlama	Bangarrinji	Bangarrinya
Bangarrinji	Yakamarina	Jiyanaku	Niwanama
Jukudayi	Nangala	Balyarrinji	Balyarrinya
Balyarrinji	Nimarama	Jukudayi	Nulanyma
Jurulaku	Niwanama	Jamaraku	Nimarama
Jangalaku	Nulanyma	Yakamari	Yakamarina
Yakamari	Bangarrinya	Jangalaku	Nangala

Source: *Carpentaria Downs/Balbirini Land Claim No. 160: Report and recommendation of the former Aboriginal Land Commissioner, Justice Gray, to the Minister for Aboriginal and Torres Strait Islander Affairs and to the Administrator of the Northern Territory*, Canberra, Aboriginal and Torres Strait Islander Commission, 1999.

It is worth noting here that despite claims that many Aboriginal communities do not traditionally have the vocabulary to count beyond three, this organisation illustrates a different type of mathematics, one that is not often understood by non-Aboriginal folk but certainly one that is highly complex. Simply because a vocabulary is seemingly not present does not mean that ideas and concepts cannot or do not exist in different ways. And this cyclic system of social organisation protected, for thousands of years, the small populations of Aboriginal peoples from genetic damage through marriages that were too close.

Our kinship/skin groups represent the mathematics of logic but also other things that have grown within the context of Aboriginal Australian cultures because that is what was necessary to sustain the small populations of peoples within different nation groups. There is significant other knowledge, too, beyond what I speak about here, sitting in this social organisation of communities that can be told by Elders.

The next way of relationship is through clan, which places a person in larger family groups. Gudanji have several clans: I am Rrumbarriya clan. Through both skin and clan groups I am also related to those other groups within the Gulf of Carpentaria and Barkly Tableland region.

Then there is relationship through the creation time and the songlines. Dreaming stories and songlines link my name, and therefore me, to the greater Gudanji context and geographic environment. Songlines represent the presence of kujiga, which immediately connects individuals to place.

My name, Pbirrianjulunga, links me to our central creation story and its related songline of three water women who left the ocean and travelled. They came ashore in the Gulf of Carpentaria, then journeyed across land to the north of Gudanji Country proper and travelled down towards what is now known as the central Northern

Territory. As they arrived at the edge of the desert region, they turned to head north-east until they arrived at Garranjini, which is the birthplace of Gudanji and an important site in the Marumbarna songline. This songline is an important travelling story that is shared by several groups in the Gulf and Tableland country. Through these stories my kujiga is linked with sites on Country in ways that are different to the connectedness with Country I have through general living activity. This difference is an integral one and reflects real responsibilities to people, place and ceremony.

So, for Gudanji, naming is a complex process of bringing an individual into pre-existing responsibility to Country sites, family groups and to others through skin, to even more others through clans and to still more others through our creation stories and songlines. These initial processes of relationship form some of the primary ways of relationship within Gudanji community. Although this is all relevant, particularly for Gudanji people within my clan and skin group, it also has connotations for many others.

We exist through our names, which are concerned with extended community. Names and naming are a central social organiser and social control mechanism within Gudanji community. Unlike Western understandings of naming and the search for unique and individual names, Gudanji are very aware that we ‘borrow’ names for the short period of time our life force is *on* Country, and we have a responsibility to keep those names safe, healthy and well during our stewardship. Significantly, when Gudanji ask someone their bush name, it is the same as asking about bush medicine. Naming, through songlines, skin and clan, contributes to the wellbeing of individuals, forming a network of 'good medicine' across Country, constructing wellness. This knowledge forms the most basic way of how we live in connection to other entities we are in kin with. This knowledge becomes more complex and layered as a person ages and responsibilities grow into Elder status.

Embedded within Gudanji practice are the three essentials of reciprocity, obligation and responsibility. Within my community, if individuals work at and achieve these three big ideas, they have little need of worry for their rights – the rights of everyone are assured. Our community has always been concerned with collectivism. It is not individualism that provides a safe and nurturing community for all; individuals can too easily lose sight of their importance and significance in the broader human condition.

The collective self in a research practice

Mankujba is a Gudanji word that refers to ways of hearing, listening, thinking, feeling and remembering, either individually or simultaneously. In research terms, it allows for collaboration between different methods, enhances the potential to expose new knowledge and makes it possible to render a multiplicity of meanings and ways of knowing garnered through a range of authors and stories. This process also depends on an awareness and understanding of the mechanisms of meaning-making specific to Gudanji peoples, but which is likely to be also common in the practices of other First Nations Australians.

Through the academic work of my First Nations predecessors, my researcher Elders, both nationally and internationally, I was gifted the opportunity to work in this way. I hope that my research and how I present it here helps to address the ongoing impact of past and sometimes present practices of colonial injustices, which continue to silence Aboriginal Australian peoples and make our ways invisible or located in the shadows.

My original research practice included interviews through Gudanji wurdijirrimi wurlun mirra, or sitting in a circle, and marranya, or sharing stories, diarising and journalling. I also engaged in weaving, string making and coolamon making as memory-aiding events to summon a shared past that placed me in a culturally responsible and respectful present. For me as a Gudanji woman, these activities of creating string and baskets and wooden dishes constitute a key making process that ensures the continuity of our community. And for six months, with the financial support of Deakin University, I lived on Country, where I collected and prepared food and walked across the same landscapes as my ancestors. I also visited specific sites to recall events and activities, invoking relationships through that past–present–future-making narrative practice with my Country acting as a reminder and a mnemonic.

When conducting my research, I followed the protocols of being on Country. They dictated all my activity while I was there. It was essential that, as a Gudanji person, daughter, sister, aunt, grandmother and mother, I respectfully observed the relationships that exist, and that are interpreted and taught to us by the Elders, between Country and us as Gudanji people. I was obliged to be aware of my presence on Country and how that affected

Country, others and entities, our relationships and our interconnectedness often told through our birth into skin groups but taught also by the community. I followed Gudanji law as given to Gudanji people since the time of the Ancestors' creation, and encompassing the present time.

And so here we are

As members of this new Australian nation together, it is imperative that we start to see the complexity and complications that have arisen through Aboriginal living with this place. I know that, for many, the framing of Aboriginal ways through theoretical discourse will not be comfortable and will in fact cause confusion. That is a good thing. It is time to disrupt a very erroneous narrative that started here when Cook claimed Country that was never his or open for claiming. We need to begin the business of being able to at least communicate a little more effectively and I hope I have shown enough reason as to why it is important that we choose the words we use with care and consideration. This was never an empty land. It was not without its human and non-human inhabitants who had long ago learned that to live unwisely was not a good idea. Abusing each other, and the natural environment, is not conducive to anyone's wellbeing.

I hope, too, that Aboriginal people's connection to Country has been clarified a little further. It is only through our ways and definitions that the fullness of this vital relationship can be told. I hope that I have furthered knowledge of the real and arcane relationships that identify Country as a truly and deeply significant life form. I have spoken only from a standpoint specific to verbal communication through a semiotic framing. I know there is much more work to be done.

English is a wonderful language but its role in the colonisation of people and places locates it in a very insidious position. It is a language that has travelled far, that had its birth on the other side of the world, and it deserves our attention and care. That birth was for people who have also travelled far from their place of heritage and identity, and in its modern form English is only 700 years old, but now we must be involved in the work of helping it grow. It has remained too unevolved in its use and engagement with its new geographic environment and the people and entities of this place. The assumption of its ability and right to be used in the way it has been here in Australia must be corrected.

I do not reject the English language. It has become mine, but it is not mine in the way that my first language is. I speak its vocabulary in ways that are shaped by the meaning- and sense-making ways of a Gudanji and Wakaja person. I do not speak poor English, merely an Australian version, as I suspect most other Australians, Aboriginal or otherwise, do.

I want to offer my sincere respect here to those members of the Aboriginal community who were removed in the first round of the Stolen Generations particularly. I want to acknowledge the position of linguistic deprivation in which they were placed. As children not allowed to speak their language, and torn from their families and communities, they endured something truly horrific. They became truly voiceless. Imagine abruptly losing your language, being beaten if you spoke it and then being educated to a year three or four level in a foreign language. I hope this book identifies some of your experience and language memories and honours your persistence in rebuilding yourself and your family.

Aboriginal Australian ways are not part of the dominant knowledge and related systems because we are still viewed, mostly kindly but not always, through a lens that renders us simple and basic. And that view arose mostly because of the awful labelling of terra nullius. We, Aboriginal peoples, have lived and practised one of the oldest and longest-lasting civilisations in the world – and we continue to do so. To deeply appreciate and understand the cultural differences between the first and the newer Australians, a fresh type of truth telling is required – one that shows the dangers and limitations of one culture assuming its ability to articulate or translate another. This singularity in thinking does not understand that cultural differences are simply that and do not reflect or represent any hierarchical value, intelligence or superior capacity of dominant cultures. All Australians have value, and difference is not in any way deficiency.

The First Peoples possess significant knowledge and practice that has the potential to contribute to our nation, this place now called Australia, in real and salient ways. The sheer longevity of living here has meant truly long practice and learning through action until those at least 280 communities got it right and were able to live well in ways that are only now becoming known to other Australians.

Thanks

I find myself in the wild position of finalising for publication book number two and, even wilder, a third book not so far away. Wild, because writing for the public was neither planned nor imagined and I am certainly intimately more aware now of the back story of literature and its production.

Some of the characters in the back story of this book include my editor, Anna Rogers. Anna, as editor, was recently described as maestro, and it is a well-deserved label.

The team at Echo Publishing, led by the extraordinary Juliet Rogers, have again provided a context where I concern myself with the words and they take care of all else. The scope of their work, their care, their support and the gracious energy of Juliet and her staff is truly outstanding.

I spent time working on this manuscript specifically

through the generous support of Helen Stacey-Bunton and Dr David Bunton and the Pirku murititya UniSA Visiting Research Fellowship at the University of South Australia in 2023. I deeply appreciate Helen's and David's kindness and warmth in hosting my visit to their home, introducing me to some of the Strathalbyn community and sharing their vast knowledge of and passion for a beautiful part of South Australia.

Thank you to Sue Joseph for your friendship and guidance and ears and willingness to read and offer feedback, and to Antonia Pont for your belief in my thinking.

Thank you to the wonderful Evelyn Araluen for her generous comments on her reading of *Terraglossia*. An extraordinary poet and scholar, her thoughts are deeply appreciated.

My daughter Ryhia (@nardurna) has again created the beautiful cover design for this book – thank you, sweetheart. And as always and forever, Rick, thank you. Teke, Ryhia, Karl, Drisana and Johnnie, you inspire me every day. I love you.

Also by Debra Dank

We come with this place

(Echo Publishing, 2022)

Shortlisted for the 2023 Prime Minister's Award for Non-Fiction

2023 New South Wales Premier's Literary Awards:

- Winner of the Douglas Stewart Prize for Non-Fiction
- Winner of the Indigenous Writers' Prize
- Winner of the UTS Glenda Adams Award for New Writing
- Winner, Book of the Year

Winner of the 2023 Australian Literature Society Gold Medal

DR DEBRA DANK

2023 Queensland Literary Awards:

- Winner of the University of Queensland Non-Fiction Book Award
- Shortlisted for the Queensland Premier's Award for a Work of State Significance
- Shortlisted for *The Courier-Mail* People's Choice Queensland Book of the Year Award

Shortlisted for the 2023 Stella Prize

2022 Prime Minister's Summer Reading List, Grattan Institute

Praise for *We come with this place*

‘This is a heart-stopping voyage into bush Aboriginal life, philosophy and history. Dank’s grandmother was a Law Boss for her Gudanji Country; her father literally ran for his life from frontier violence. Her [recollection] of growing up on remote Queensland cattle stations, drinking from sacred hidden rock-wells, educated by correspondence school and living in a caravan it was illegal for her Aboriginal parents to own, will surprise, delight and astound you.’

– Melissa Lucashenko, *Sydney Morning Herald*

‘an unheralded reflection on what it is to be First Nations in Australia, and on the very deepest meanings of family and belonging … exemplifies all that First Nations writing can and should be. The writing is culturally rigorous and deeply thoughtful. Dank seeks to expand the horizons of the reader in a way which centres, not the author as an individual, but rather her Country and the wider community she has grown within. Most of all, her [narrative] shows a powerful path forward from colonial trauma towards a space of mutual respect and self-determining futures. Essential reading.’

– Judging panel, 2023 NSW Premier’s Literary Award

‘*We Come with This Place* is deeply personal, a profound tribute to family and the Gudanji Country to which Debra Dank belongs, but it is much more than that. Here is Australia as it has been for countless generations, land and people in effortless balance, and Australia as it became, but also Australia as it could and should be.’

– Judging panel, 2023 Stella Prize

‘this is a book to lean into and take time with. Foremost, this is a story to learn from. In her introduction, Dank calls it “a strange kind of letter, written to my place”, and yet that strange weaving back and forth through time and dimension adds to the reader’s experience. *We Come with This Place* is a jewel of a book, one Australians in particular ought to read and refer to …’

– Tara June Winch

‘A wonderfully illuminating account of what it is to be a fully successful contributor to our world, but to be alive as well in one that we know too little about. Here, though, we are invited to enter and feel its groundedness and abiding richness.’

– David Malouf

‘As Australia contemplates a Voice to Parliament, this book reminds us to listen. Listen when the land tells her story. Hear the voices of the traditional owners. Listen first and then you will know.’

– 2022 Prime Minister’s Summer Reading List,
Grattan Institute